Academy of One

Academy of One

The Power and Promise of Open-Source Learning

David Preston

ROWMAN & LITTLEFIELD
Lanham • Boulder • New York • London

Published by Rowman & Littlefield
An imprint of The Rowman & Littlefield Publishing Group, Inc.
4501 Forbes Boulevard, Suite 200, Lanham, Maryland 20706
www.rowman.com

6 Tinworth Street, London SE11 5AL, United Kingdom

British Library Cataloguing in Publication Information Available

Library of Congress Cataloging-in-Publication Data

Names: Preston, David, 1970– author.
Title: Academy of one : the power and promise of open-source learning / David Preston.
Description: Lanham, Maryland : Rowman & Littlefield, 2021. | Includes bibliographical
    references and index. | Summary: "Academy of One introduces readers
    to open-source Learning, the model that transforms education for the
    Information Age"—Provided by publisher.
Identifiers: LCCN 2020046471 (cloth) | LCCN 2020951049 (paper) |
    LCCN 2020046472 (ebook) | ISBN 9781475859041 (cloth) |
    ISBN 9781475859058 (paper) | ISBN 9781475859065 (epub)
Subjects: LCSH: Open learning. | Open educational resources. | Education—Effect of
    technological innovations on.
Classification: LCC LC5800 .P74 2021 (print) | LCC LC5800 (ebook) |
    DDC 374/.4—dc23
LC record available at https://lccn.loc.gov/2020046471
LC ebook record available at https://lccn.loc.gov/2020046472

♾™ The paper used in this publication meets the minimum requirements of American
National Standard for Information Sciences—Permanence of Paper for Printed Library
Materials, ANSI/NISO Z39.48-1992.

Dedication
My wife Haley stops us on the trail, delighted, to lean down and reveal the secrets of flowers. Through her wisdom, I experience the beauty and medicine and stories that were waiting right there in front of me all along.

My daughter Tara can find a rainbow at night. Through her unclouded perception, I experience the humor and hope and curiosity that only appear when you look with your heart.

This book is a love letter to learning, and all of our teachers.

*It is dedicated
to the sweet, fascinated little girl within Haley who holds close and remembers,
and
to the strong, talented woman Tara envisions
becoming—may she never forget.*

Contents

Foreword

Scary—But Worth It

Howard Rheingold

Howard Rheingold is a futurist, educator, and author who coined the term and wrote the book on Virtual Community. *Rheingold also wrote* Smart Mobs, Net Smart, *and other prescient works that accurately predicted the trends and influences of digital technologies on our society and culture— decades ahead of their time. Rheingold taught at Stanford University and the University of California Berkeley.*

Thank you, Mrs. Burch, for igniting my passion for learning by starting me out with something I was already eager to learn.

Although sixty years have passed, I still remember the name and face of the fifth grade teacher who cared enough to start our educational relationship with an activity I personally cared about. Mrs. Burch and what she did for me came to mind again in 2011 when I learned about David Preston and his revolutionary strategy of trusting students to take their learning seriously when they centered it on their own interests.

I had some serious trouble in the fifth grade. The first teacher I had that year hated me. Granted, I was probably a smartass, and definitely a redhead with a mischievous look on my face. But to this day I believe she didn't like me because I knew more than she did about some things and was unabashedly vocal about it. She actually dunced me—made me sit in a corner, facing the wall. I was so unhappy that, instead of walking to school the next day, I sat in the orange grove behind our house reading science fiction.

Of course, this lasted only one day. When my parents and I were summoned to the principal's office, my parents insisted that I wasn't the problem (thank you, parents!). They transferred me to another school.

When I arrived at the new school and reported to Mrs. Burch's classroom, she immediately took me aside and told me that her class published a "newspaper," a mimeographed three-sheet collection of articles about what was going on around school.

"We are approaching deadline," Mrs. Burch told me, "and we need someone to interview the principal right away. Would you like to do that?" I still remember that when the principal asked if I needed him to spell "principal" for me, I told him I had it covered. And I remember that he was impressed. Interesting that I remember very little else about the fifth grade, but the day in the orange grove and the interview with the principal still stand out so crisply in my memory.

Did Mrs. Burch perceive (or learn from my mother, also a teacher) that I had an interest in writing? Or did she ignite it? In any case, she hit the bulls-eye: I have spent my entire working life as a writer, in tandem with ten years as a teacher. It's not possible to determine whether or not that day channeled me into a writing career, but without a doubt it remains my most vivid positive recollection of my elementary school years.

That class, that day, and its significance reverberated in my memory again when I first encountered David Preston. I was teaching at Stanford at the time and dropped in on the Institute for the Future, which was just down the street from campus, in time to hear Dr. Preston's presentation on his vision for "Open-Source Learning."

At the time I met David, I was working for the MacArthur Foundation-funded "Digital Media and Learning" website, conducting interviews with innovators in education. In my interview with David (see page 150), he talked about "hacking the curriculum" by inviting his students to co-design their syllabus and encouraging them to use digital media—blogs, videos, videoconference interviews, collaborative documents—to explore topics that they chose. In addition to interest-based learning and digital media, David encouraged metacognitive learning by challenging students to examine how they were going about learning.

Trusting students to take over some of the responsibility for their learning is scary for teachers. Scary because of a fear that students will act irresponsibly if not tightly constrained, and scary because principals are expected to be skeptical.

When I encountered this fear during my three years of interviewing educators, I was happy to point them to David Preston. My own teaching was also transformed: I began to call my college students "co-learners." It seemed like a minor semantic tactic before I did it, but I quickly learned that when a teacher authorizes cooperation around mutual learning, the learners take it seriously.

I invited co-learner teams of three to co-teach with me, taking responsibility for leading learning activities and discussions for one-third of our class time. My fears were replaced by enthusiasm when students proved to be more than trustworthy—in every case, they grew more and more enthusiastic as they learned how they could apply our learning objectives to their own interests.

If I have a regret as a teacher, it's that I didn't trust my students more radically earlier in my teaching career.

During the last course I taught at Stanford, after the first three sessions, I wrote in blue on the whiteboard all of the learning activities I required: forum posts, blog posts, co-teaching teams, collaborative lexicon building, and individual projects. Then I wrote my phone number on the whiteboard and told them I was going to walk around campus while they re-engineered the required learning activities to fit their own requirements. They could text me with questions, then text me when they were ready for me to return. I had a few questions, and after forty-five minutes I was invited to return.

The co-learners had revised, in red marker, the list of required learning activities. We talked about why they preferred these changes (bringing in the metacognitive element of student-centered pedagogy), then ran the course that way. I wish I had not waited until my final course to try this! In an ideal world, I would meet with co-learners for several hours online and offline before the course is scheduled to start, and they could help co-design my draft syllabus.

We are fortunate that David has laid out how and why this student-centric learning works, how digital media can enhance collaborative project-based learning, and how to go about applying what David learned through his own brave rethinking of trust, responsibility, interest, and collaboration in high school classrooms. I won't be surprised when elementary and college level teachers begin experimenting.

As a fellow teacher, I encourage you to build at least some of the required learning—sources, skills, principles, methods—around projects that enlist learners' enthusiasm. Let them know they are both trusted and expected to be responsible. Encourage them to understand how they learn most effectively and why.

Yes, it's scary. And yes, the payoff is worth it.

Preface

A Note to Start

Conversations about education can get messy. In today's world, it can be hard to know what works, and even harder to know how to inspire change.

Let's create some clarity.

The pages that follow describe how you can use Open-Source Learning to pursue your own teaching interests and goals; create and curate learning journeys in ways that produce value, interdependence, and hope; and connect with others around the world to form learning alliances that help and inspire.

I wish that we could take our time and thoughtfully develop a systemic approach to changing education, but that simply isn't the way things work. Evolution is not a gradual process or a matter of strategic planning; if the water rises, the very next generation must either swim and breathe underwater, or die. In today's world, the realities of poverty, violence, and disease are disrupting life at school and forcing us all to reexamine our learning practices in order to survive and thrive.

As I write this note, I am sheltered at home during the coronavirus pandemic. The courses I teach are running much the same way they have for years, but my students and I—along with everyone else—are operating under a massive amount of uncertainty and stress. Now more than ever, learners need healing, resilience, and hope. The water is rising.

Many of the ideas that you will explore here defy the conventional. Some dig into belief systems and thought processes we don't normally slow down to consider. Now is the perfect time for reflection. The conventional approaches that have brought us this far will bring us no farther. The potential results are worth the risk, and the current risks demand that we seek better results.

I have taught at every level of formal education, elementary, middle, and high school in Los Angeles and California's central coast, graduate school at UCLA, and elsewhere. My experiences, research, and collaborations along the way have taught me one thing above all else: trusting students to participate in the creation of the learning process is the surest way to create profound opportunities and outcomes.

The next generation of students in America will amplify and accelerate their learning by using digital tools and methods, along with time-honored best practices, to transform their work in ways that the generations before them could never even imagine. This book shares examples, cases, and a framework for how you can be the catalyst for their achievements.

The ideas and practices I describe in this book are by no means the last word on Open-Source Learning—they are intended as the beginning of a conversation for all of us. My goal is to engage you in participating in an education movement for the Information Age.

Remember, this is *Open-Source* Learning—every idea here is yours for the taking. Please adopt the ones that appeal to you and make them your own. Customize them so that they work better. And then tell the world about it, so that we can learn from you too. Sharing ideas and learning with each other is the way we will build a better future.

In that spirit, I invite you to contact me with your questions, ideas, comments, or criticism. I look forward to hearing from you.

—D. P.
david@davidpreston.net

Prologue

TAKING OFF: ACHIEVING THE IMPOSSIBLE

Given the will, we have the capacity to achieve the impossible.
Eddie Rickenbacker, American World War I Ace

It's a bad idea to start the day on social media. But there I was, at 4:30 a.m. on a Sunday morning, reading the tweet from Matt Reynolds. For the third time.

@prestonlearning—good morning for a flight?
Oh wait, still a little early.

I'd been looking forward to this for months, but now I felt an icy tingle of fear. I replied:

@mattrey17—yes!
How many high school teachers get to tag along while a student flies a plane?
I hope this isn't my last tweet.

Flying an airplane is a long way from sitting in a typical high school classroom. Riding in the back seat while a teenager flies a plane is a long way from normal.

I read Matt's tweet again, put on a jacket, and headed out into the dark.

Ever since my daughter Tara was old enough to toddle around the kitchen and dump a cup of flour into a mixing bowl, Sunday in our house has been Pancake Sunday. I wouldn't miss Pancake Sunday for anything—so the night before, when I said goodnight to Tara, I promised her that Pancake Sunday would begin as soon as I got home from my plane ride.

A Piper Tri-Pacer airplane weighs about 2,000 pounds. When I think of things that fly through the air, a ton of metal does not make the list. The very appeal of flight is that it poses a counterintuitive challenge that divides humanity into two groups: (1) those who dare to explore the unknown and (2) those who don't. This is the mindset that separates the dreamers from the cynics, the builders from the skeptics.

It seems like whenever someone has a really interesting new idea, there is always someone around who is sure it won't work. As the story goes, when the editor of the newspaper in Dayton, Ohio, heard that the town's favorite sons, Wilbur and Orville Wright, got their first flight off the ground, he reportedly responded, "Man will never fly. And if he does, he will never come from Dayton."[1]

The kind of people who want to fly a plane take that sort of comment as motivation. They are driven by the discipline of dauntless, passionate practice. Their learning is not motivated by a grade or external approval, but by a deeper, internal source, and the satisfaction it brings.

That level of commitment is the "X" factor in the results of a person's efforts in everything we do. A handcrafted sweater. Fine food. Brilliant music. Care may not show up in a test score or a paycheck, it may not be something you can see or count, but you know it's there and it makes all the difference. There is nothing like experiencing the work product of someone who genuinely loves what they do.

People who care also inspire us through their very existence. They have overcome challenges, made mistakes, and emerged from the fire intact. They give us hope for preserving our own integrity and sense of self.

In school, the appearance of such inspiring personalities is a rarity that exposes the more conventional state of things. Part of the reason that these characters are so impressive is the intense social pressure to conform to an institutional way of thinking. School and entry-level jobs tend to neutralize the sort of commitment that leads to excellence; as a result, people learn how to play the game and appear obedient. They do just enough in class to stay out of trouble. They learn to avoid risk and making mistakes. They stop speaking up for themselves.

Anything interesting or fun in life can be distorted into something boring in school. Education policy and classroom teaching are focused on institutional outcomes, not individual learning. The K-12 educational system as we know it promotes organizational school vision statements that champion abstract ideas like *safe, nurturing, potential,* and *future*—all worthwhile concepts indeed, but not ones that stir the blood or dare a young person to embark on a learning adventure.

School's ongoing quest for relevance and respectability has led the public discussion of education policy to focus on what can be measured. It's hard to quantify and document invisible qualities such as engagement, care, love, or resilience, so K-12 schools emphasize what's observable: test scores, grades, and outward behaviors. Unfortunately, analyzing these sorts of surface-impression metrics doesn't help us understand how well students learn, or what they learn, or how education can encourage life-fulfilling experiences. Checking your watch doesn't tell you anything about the physics of time.

These factors create a school culture that can suffocate a young person who wants to become a pilot.

* * *

I met Matt in an English class I taught for high school seniors that was listed in the course catalog as "Expository Reading & Writing Course." WestEd, the education research agency, described the course this way: "The Expository Reading and Writing Course (ERWC) was developed by California State University (CSU) faculty and high school educators to improve the academic literacy of high school seniors, thereby reducing the need for students to enroll in remedial English courses when they enter college."[2]

Matt had to take an English course as a requirement for graduation; he was taking this particular course because he was applying to attend San Jose State, a CSU campus.

Matt was pleasant enough. We said hello most days. He was never obnoxious or threatening. But even though he wanted to attend college, Matt quietly refused to do the coursework. While other students were online writing or doing research, I watched as Matt played video games or checked social media on his phone.

The phone wasn't the problem. I encourage students to use their phones or tablets in class, and I gave Matt space to make decisions about how to use his time—and, he made it obvious that he had better things to do with his time. To help Matt connect the dots, I introduced his class to some ideas about motivation and resiliency. I focused on the difference between the things we have to do versus the things we get to do.

Students in school often adopt the mentality of incarcerated prisoners. It is important to understand this attitude as a coping mechanism because it can shape individual experiences and influence the entire classroom culture.

If a person can survive a Holocaust concentration camp and teach others to thrive, I reasoned, he has something valuable to offer anyone who feels trapped, so I introduced Matt and his classmates to the work of Victor Frankl, the Austrian neurologist and psychiatrist who authored *Man's Search for Meaning*, in which he wrote: "Any attempt to restore a man's inner strength in the camp had first to succeed in showing him some future goal. Nietzsche's words, 'Those who have a *why* to live, can bear with almost any *how*,' could be the guiding motto for all psychotherapeutic and psychohygienic efforts regarding prisoners."[3]

I told the students the truth: no matter what I taught, it might not appeal to everyone, so if anyone had a better idea about what they wanted to learn, I was willing to listen.

It is difficult to accurately gauge a student's understanding or skill level when the student's work product is a rushed afterthought; an essay from a student who is struggling to learn English may have the same number of errors and ill-conceived conclusions as a paper from an exceptionally capable student who understands the task and simply doesn't get around to doing the work until just before the bell rings.

We learn best when we're fully engaged, when we love what we're doing so much that it doesn't feel like work and we lose track of time, when we feel so joyfully determined that we even embrace our mistakes, because they teach us and inspire us to keep going and improve.

If we are going to learn—as opposed to just being taught—we need to develop this as a form of fitness, just like anything else we want to strengthen or do well. As a starting point, students need to be allowed, encouraged, and empowered to find out what it is they really want to learn about. That's the thing they're going to dedicate themselves to in a way that shows the rest of us what their best really looks like.

That goal is worthwhile but seldom achieved. By the time most students are in high school, they have been trained to stop asking questions and conditioned to follow instructions. They are resigned to being told what to do, and they are increasingly immune to even the mere suggestion that anything else is possible. Students are accustomed to opening-day promises from teachers about how courses will be exciting, creative, and different. They have been let down before and they no longer believe the hype.

So, first, students have to trust that the offer to create their own learning path is genuine. Then the hard work begins. Today's students are so busy and stressed out by trying to meet all of their obligations that it can be difficult for them to imagine allocating more of their time and energy to something that isn't a chore, part of their job, or a typical school "assignment" that gets them points.

With all of this in mind, I offered Matt's class a choice. For the win, if they believed in such a thing, and for the grade, for the cynics who needed the guarantee of an external incentive. As an alternative to the dreaded textbook-based coursework, I invited each student to develop an individual Big Question (more on this in chapter 2). I asked them to think about what they really wanted to know. Then I asked them to imagine how the resources available on campus and elsewhere could help them.

We brainstormed with one goal in mind: find something to learn about— a skill, an idea, a question, a potential career, anything—that you can care about enough to do your best.

The students were understandably skeptical. They had learned that if something seems too good to be true, it probably is. Matt posted to his blog:

Honestly, for me high school is a waste of time. It was created many, many years ago and is taught pretty much the same way ever since it was created. If schools want kids to do well and not slack, then teach them what they want to know. I plan on majoring in Aviation Operations. Nothing in high school is going to really prepare me for what's going to happen after I graduate and get into college. And isn't that what the whole purpose of a High School is for—to prepare you for the next level of education? I agree—I can be lazy and a slacker and do the bare minimum. But if you give me something that I like and can use in the real world, then I'll knock your freakin' socks off. And I think that's the problem today. School is run the same way as always. Fix this and you fix the problem.[4]

I took Matt at his word and commented to his post:

Fair points. And, now that you can select a curriculum that you like and can use in the real world, my socks are waiting . . .

* * *

Often lost in the discussion of low achievement in schools is the simple reality that most students are not lazy—they are just not inspired. Students crave the opportunity to seek experiences that are interesting or valuable to them as individuals, and they want room to explore so that they can discover what's most meaningful or rewarding.

I took Matt's post as great news. Unlike students who had never really asked themselves what they really wanted, Matt had figured it out. He was dedicated to learning about flight and literally getting himself off the ground.

When I learned that Matt really wanted to fly airplanes, his approach to school made more sense. Matt knew he needed to pass my course to graduate. But high school has no courses about aircraft, no planes, and no tolerance for students who don't play the game. So, Matt was biding his time, doing just enough to not fail while sneaking peeks at flight-related websites and simulators on his phone, waiting to get out there and get on with his life.

* * *

When it comes to developing specialty skills and content, the best mentors are usually found outside the classroom. This is one of many reasons why it is important to learn early about our needs, and the people and the information that can help us meet those needs.

Open-Source Learning teaches students how to find the experts and the expertise they need, and how to apply that knowledge to their specific interests and goals. The internet has given us the opportunity to reach out to anyone and connect around every conceivable interest.

I model this concept so that students can see me learn as well. I seek out experts and I incorporate what I learn from them into my professional and personal practices. This provides an example for students to follow as they seek out knowledgeable mentors in their own lives.

Once Matt got clear on what he needed, and he reflected on the experts and potential mentors in his life, he didn't have to look any further than his own brother's father-in-law.

Ed Mandibles is an engineer with a long-time love of flying. Ed proposed to his wife at 3000 feet in a single-engine Piper. Ed became the president of a Piper club that every July draws hundreds of pilots and planes to the Lompoc Airport for a flyers' festival.

The first thing Ed told me when I met him is that what he loves most about flying is sharing his passion with other people. Ed's children have flown his plane, and now his grandchildren do. Like many pilots and others who have a deep understanding of the physical universe, Ed is totally down-to-earth and insatiably curious; just spending time and talking with the guy leads to insights that are both inspiring and educational.

When I met Ed, he covered so many topics in just a few minutes: family, travel, and the comparative risks of exposure to nuclear radiation versus a day at the beach without sunscreen. He showed me the bicycles he was building for friends to get around the airport. Ed not only had a plane and the skills to teach Matt to be a pilot—he had a tank full of passionate curiosity. This was fuel that could accelerate Matt's learning.

Sharing passion for curiosity itself is a powerful amplifier in the learning process. Why aren't more students curious, you ask? Often, it is *precisely* because they are good learners. Students understand school as the institutional arm of a culture that punishes curiosity. Curiosity killed the cat. Icarus flew too close to the sun. Eve ate the forbidden fruit of the tree of knowledge of good and evil. Obedience is the path to reward, and school is where this message is reinforced.

Obedience training isn't going to help you fly a plane. During any given moment of flight, a pilot draws upon knowledge from a variety of domains: physics, mathematics, communication skills, geometry, even philosophy and spirituality. "When you see the world from the air," Ed told me, "you find yourself thinking on a more cosmic scale."

Choosing Ed as a mentor was a wise decision on Matt's part. Ed not only provided Matt with access to a plane and thorough instruction about how to fly; he shared a sense of enthusiasm and wonder that led to all sorts of intellectual connections and discoveries. Without saying as much, Ed was modeling and teaching Matt how to be a thinker and a lover of learning. Watching Ed and Matt work together was the perfect illustration of what schools like to call "lifelong learning."

This, then, was Matt's "why." Whether or not Matt was destined to become a professional pilot, the desire to fly could fuel Matt's learning, his success in high school, in college, and his sense of potential for the rest of his life. So I worked with Matt to completely redesign his experience in our course. Matt began reading and writing about the history, physics, and career opportunities of flight, and his work product showed how much he cared about his subject.

So it was that, just three months after I first read Matt's blog post, there I was, reading and rereading that tweet and leaving home on Pancake Sunday to go on a potential suicide mission with two people who could easily be mistaken for a high schooler with an attitude problem and his elderly relative.

I admit that I had second thoughts: *Why did I ever agree to this? Why am I putting my life in the hands of a retired hobbyist and a . . . TEENAGER?*

In full view of my fears, I savored the moment. I consciously decided to trust Matt. He was earnest, and I had seen him change as he learned from an expert. I saw the shift in the way he focused and took pride in his work. I observed him pay attention to detail and completely shut out the distractions he had so enthusiastically pursued just weeks earlier. When I read his writing or listened to him answer questions about aviation, I could tell he was thinking deeply and understanding, not just faking his way through the subject matter.

* * *

It was still dark when I pulled into the high school parking lot that Sunday morning. Matt was already there, waiting for me. I locked my car, walked over to Matt's Honda, and opened the passenger door. I figured letting him drive to the airport was a sensible first step.

When we arrived at Lompoc Airport, I watched Matt closely. He walked around the aircraft, following Ed's lead. As Matt went through the pre-flight checklist, I mentally checked off the theories and methods he demonstrated that don't show up in the box score of a standardized test: Socratic method? Check. Project-based learning? Check. Explicit direct instruction? Check. Language acquisition and code switching? Check. Behaviorism? Operant conditioning? Multiple modalities and intelligences? Multiple intelligences? Check, check, check, and check. Even the "new and improved" Common Core standards: communication, collaboration, critical thinking, creativity. . . . It was all there.

It was a beautiful learning picture viewed through any lens. Most importantly, Matt was as calm and focused as a Zen monk. He was in a state of flow. He knew exactly what he was doing and why.

His checklist complete, Matt walked around to where I was standing and opened the door of the plane. "Alright, Dr. Preston," he said with a huge grin. "Time to get in the plane."

Two Smithsonian curators, Dr. Tom Crouch and Dr. Peter L. Jakab, who had written two previous books about the Wright Brothers, asked this question in their book *The Wright Brothers and the Invention of the Aerial Age*: "How did these two modest small businessmen, working essentially alone, with little formal or scientific training, solve a complex and demanding problem that had defied better-known experimenters for centuries?"[5]

Jakab provided the answer to a Smithsonian visitor during the centennial of the first flight. As they examined each element of the Wright Brothers' plane, Jakab said, "The Wrights saw the airplane as a system. It was not one invention, but many, and they all had to work in concert."[6]

This, too, is how Open-Source Learning got off the ground. Open-Source Learning is a coordinated system of learning and innovation that inspires students to create and manage their own educational experiences that are then amplified by sharing them online with everyone. Open-Source Learning is based on a series of guiding principles designed to empower learners to thrive in the real world. Some of the practices in Open-Source Learning are made possible by modern technology; most are timeless best practices that emerged over the millennia as humans evolved.

* * *

As we taxied down the runway, I sat behind Matt and listened to Ed give instructions over the headphones while we bounced along. In that moment I realized two things:

1. I was terrified.
2. There was no going back.

Whatever our reservations or our fears about new ways of learning in the Information Age, larger forces are carrying us toward a frontier we have not yet imagined. Learning our way through it will require courage to ask questions that our own schooling never taught us to anticipate. Open-Source Learning can provide some of the answers. As Nelson Mandela wrote, "I learned that courage was not the absence of fear, but the triumph over it. The brave man is not he who does not feel afraid, but he who conquers that fear."[7]

And then abruptly the ground dropped away beneath us, and we were aloft.

Chapter 1

It's a Crazy World Out There

It's a crazy world out there. Be curious.

Stephen Hawking[1]

In chaos, there is fertility.

Anaïs Nin[2]

We need courage to make changes in the way we teach and learn as we face an increasingly complex and uncertain future. We need courage to take the leap and abandon the old ways in favor of the new.

It's a leap we have to take. Baby steps will not get us where we need to go.

The sky is not the limit. It's not even close. Matt Reynolds's story only seems exceptional because school is so limited and our expectations are so low. His achievement is exactly the sort of thing that happens when we think more expansively and encourage every learner to explore the possibilities.

We have to think bigger than school. School does not prepare young people for the world of the future—or even of today—by teaching "the standardized curriculum but on computers" on campuses where practices are so obsolete that the computer lab furniture is arranged according to medieval-era interior design principles and students graduate without being able to define or explain the word "internet."

For all its limitations, school is a strong belief system that has limited and shaped our imagination about learning for centuries. To the extent that we can recover our power to be curious, to ask questions, and to reimagine how we can support the next generation of learners, we can contribute to this belief system in a meaningful way so that education institutions become more responsive to the needs of learners at this point in history or, at least, so that learners can more effectively use the resources in that massive infrastructure to their own advantage.

To this point, even though digital culture has advanced by leaps and bounds, the power and capabilities of the internet have been strangled by our current system of education. The organizational structure, financial incentives, and political culture of "school" are so forceful that they have bent the internet and online tools to fit the shape of an old-fashioned classroom. As a result, education technology now looks like digitized textbooks, screen-based testing platforms, walled garden portfolios, and "learning management systems."

The internet is not a tool or a toy. As author, activist, and Electronic Frontier Foundation board member Cory Doctorow put it, "We live in a world of computers. The internet is the nervous system of the 21st century."[3]

For this reason among others, computers are not just another academic subject. Seymour Papert, the MIT mathematician and philosopher who created the Logo programming language and helped educators reimagine the computer as an instrument for creative thinking, put the idea this way: "Our goal in education should be to foster the ability to use the computer in everything you do," said Papert, "even if you don't have a specific piece of software for the job."

"Often kids in a computer lab learn about word-processing, but if they want to write an essay, they write it by hand. This is exactly the opposite of what you want them to learn. They're approaching the computer as just another abstract school subject."[4]

The good news is that all of the features of the public internet are available right now for all of us to use. We do not need another "technology initiative" or specialized curriculum. In fact, we can transform education without asking permission or forgiveness, or by spending one extra dollar.

We can meet traditional academic standards and establish standards of intellectual and personal excellence, while simultaneously preserving learners' freedom to embark on interdisciplinary learning journeys of their own. We can create optimal conditions for growth in the garden without requiring all the flowers to be the same.

Having high standards is not the same thing as standardizing school or evaluating its effectiveness through the use of standardized tests. Encouraging each learner to achieve their fullest potential is the highest standard—and one that by definition rejects standardization. This transcends learning; it is an essential principal of personal identity, including sex, gender, age, sexual preference, race, ethnicity, and every other characteristic that gives us a sense of self that is simultaneously contextualized by uniqueness and belonging. Albert Einstein addressed this in terms of being Jewish: "Standardization robs life of its spice. To deprive every ethnic group of its special traditions is to convert the world into a huge Ford plant. I believe in standardizing automobiles. I do not believe in standardizing human beings. Standardization is a great peril which threatens American culture."[5]

For over a decade, students in Open-Source Learning networks have proven that individually created learning is the solution to a schooling world where conformity to one-size-fits-all approaches have become the problem. The effect is a more tightly knit community; encouraging individuals to explore and express unique perspectives establishes a shared value that brings us all closer together in support of a common cause.

Often, habit is the only reason for continuing mediocre practices. It's an old story in management consulting: the consultant asks a management team why they do something a certain way, the group looks around in awkward silence, and then someone says either, "Because we've always done it that way" or "We've never done it any other way." Why would a teacher design *for* a student when they have never met? They are about to spend the better part of a year getting to know each other. Why not offer the student an immediate chance to think, and in the process challenge the stereotype of an uncompromising authority figure that demands thoughtless obedience?

Designing *with* learners is easy. Begin with a question: "What interests you? What would you like to learn about?"

Then, when they say, "Can I learn about . . .?" the Open-Source Learning answer is always: "*Yes!*" This may initially feel like a loss of control that leads to anarchy, but that is not what happens. By assuming ownership and taking the first step on an interdisciplinary journey, the learner has tapped into a source of intrinsic motivation. This is the wellspring of an internal sense of discipline that will make the study of academic subjects more relevant and worthwhile.

That is when the fun begins. To move forward, however, it is important to offer some structural support, because most students are not used to this much freedom. They have been trained in a system built around rewards and punishments, and they will want to know what it means to succeed at this new game. Later chapters will provide details and examples from students. To practice, imagine any wild-hair question off the top of your head and then ask yourself:

• What academic subjects or skills will the student need to learn about in order to understand this question more deeply?

• What tools can students use to research these topics and show that they have mastered (or at least improved their understanding of) them?

Most college students do not ask very good questions during lecture and they don't visit their professors during office hours. It's hard to speak up in front of people, and it can be intimidating to sit with the expert. Apart from facilitating understanding of traditional academic subjects and exploring topics of interest, Open-Source Learning helps students develop their ability to think clearly and assert themselves in order to articulate what is important to them. Co-designing their learning experience helps next-generation learners begin to develop the self-awareness and the critical and creative thinking skills necessary to make themselves understood, identify opportunities, solve problems, and use the technology of our age to create value, interdependence, and hope.

Students produce millions of artifacts each school year that are never seen by anyone except the teacher. Curating student learning where everyone can see it—beginning with an account of the first conversation between teacher and student about what the student wants to learn—connects the value of effort with a tangible outcome. Rather than waiting for someday after graduation, Open-Source Learning encourages students to create and trade on the value of their learning in real time.

The principle of immediacy also applies to interconnectedness and collaboration. Instead of forcing students to remain isolated and wait to learn about the power of connections and networking when they eventually move into the workforce, (when they will have to recover from decades of keeping their eyes on their own paper), Open-Source Learning students learn the essential structures and processes of creating and participating in networks in order to develop communities of support and critique while they are pursuing their studies.

Perhaps most importantly, Open-Source Learning restores integrity to the idea that our learning will make tomorrow better than today. Seeing our future as a matter of possibility, and not just probability, gives us that most precious commodity of all: hope.

Every problem we see in today's environment, economy, and culture is a function of our individual and collective thinking. The survival and success of generations to come depends on the ability to learn—both independently and in connection with each other.

The chapters that follow explore the thinking behind Open-Source Learning, and how it can help you transform the fundamental processes of education in a changing world for individuals and organizations. They do so by bringing these ideas into clearer focus:

- The beliefs that underlie schooling
- How Open-Source Learning supports discovery, mastery, and retention
- How teachers introduce Open-Source Learning in the classroom
- The core values of Open-Source Learning
- The practices of Open-Source Learning networks
- Practical next steps individuals can take, whether their organizations are ready or not

Along the way, you will meet learners young and old who practice Open-Source Learning by designing, making, selecting, and improving the processes, the projects, and even the tools through which they learn. They ask interdisciplinary Big Questions that lead them to investigate multiple subjects and fields. They collaborate with each other, with teachers as expert guides, and with mentors as experts in content areas. They curate their explorations in ways that create immediate value, interdependence, and hope for themselves and others.

As you read through the concepts and examples of Open-Source Learning, you will become familiar with a conceptual framework and routines that render traditional school practices like "classroom management" obsolete. You will see how intangible qualities like empathy, trust, and vision support the efforts of learners as they become enthusiastic and engaged.

Open-Source Learning network members become diligent and resilient. They think critically and creatively. They experiment. They celebrate their mistakes as well as the "Eureka!" moments.

Some of the practices on the pages that follow may seem counterintuitive at first. For instance, teachers are not trained to walk out of the classroom and put students in charge on the first day of school.

These practices and routines of Open-Source Learning make a far greater impact than the top-down, results-oriented management style often championed by corporate executives and emulated by school administrators. So why aren't more teachers out there leading the charge?

THE NAIL THAT STICKS UP

Many innovative teachers and learners already create environments and experiences that align with the philosophy and practice of Open-Source

Learning. Too often, these individuals are considered exceptional in their own schools—and in twenty-first-century American education, the nonconformist exceptions are perceived as threatening to the conventional rule. This places some of the most successful learning innovations and practitioners at risk.

As the Japanese proverb says, "The nail that sticks up gets hammered down."[6] Most people want to fit in at school, and that includes the adults. When teachers become too popular, achieve uncommon results with students, or even look like they're having too much fun, they risk being seen as the "nail that sticks up" that others resent and look to hammer down.

Even using the word "innovative" to describe a teacher can be perceived as a backhanded compliment. The term suggests that a person or a practice is an outlier, a stray from the herd, which can make a teacher vulnerable to criticism, no matter how misguided.

If that view sounds a bit paranoid, consider, as a high-profile example, the fate of Jaime Escalante, a mathematics teacher at Garfield High School in Los Angeles. Escalante was so successful in teaching previously low-achieving students that they were accused of cheating on the Advanced Placement exam and exonerated only after being investigated and retested.

Escalante—praised by governors and presidents, featured in the 1988 film, *Stand and Deliver,* and honored on a 2016 U.S. postage stamp—was nevertheless perceived as a nail that stuck out and needed to be hammered down.

Even though Escalante's students excelled beyond any previous levels at Garfield and entered college in unprecedented numbers, Escalante's colleagues and administrators forced him out of the school because he didn't fit in or play the political game.

If you are an innovator, you are doing something unusual. At some point, you will have to explain and maybe even defend your choices. Please feel free to use the theoretical framework, proposed research agenda, and case studies in this book to reinforce your case.

School can be a lonely place when you're different. Teachers do not often get to connect with others who share their enthusiasm and ideas for innovation in education. So, this book is also an invitation for savvy practitioners to validate their work and join a like-minded professional community. Please consult the Resource section in the back of the book and visit opensourcelearning.net online.

Whether you are a teacher, a student, or you are in a learning environment outside of the educational mainstream, you can use Open-Source Learning principles to meet your teaching needs and those of your students, your family, your employees, and your community.

Throughout history, people have responded to the needs of their times by developing schools of thought and philosophies of education that they believe will empower the next generation to thrive. Now is the time for us to use Open-Source Learning to do the same.

THE LIMITATIONS OF SCHOOL DEFINE THE NEED

Leading an Open-Source Learning community in a school is like looking at the future through a dirty classroom window—it requires a well-defined vision. The traditional classroom is a closed system, isolated from the rest of the world. No one can enter or leave without a pass issued and approved by multiple gatekeepers. Work product is seen by an audience of one, papers are returned facedown, and whatever ideas and solutions they contain are crumpled in backpacks and lost to history. Grades are confidential. The teacher tells the students: "Do your own work. Keep your eyes on your own paper. Ask permission if you have to go to the bathroom."

According to Peter Gray, research professor of psychology at Boston College, "School is a place where children are compelled to be, and where their freedom is greatly restricted—far more restricted than most adults would tolerate in their workplaces. In recent decades, we have been compelling our children to spend ever more time in this kind of setting, and there is strong evidence . . . that this is causing serious psychological damage to many of them."[7]

School has never been a safe place to be vulnerable. It's hard to reveal your whole self or take intellectual risks in a place where your behavior is under close surveillance and you are constantly aware of being judged by peers and authority figures. Students want to be accepted, to be cool, to blend in with the crowd. Even raising a hand to ask a question gets a whole lot of unwanted attention.

These days, the dominance of rules, surveillance technology, tasks, and testing—not to mention the possibility of getting shot—make thinking, collaborating, and planning in school all the more difficult.

The most successful students cope not necessarily by demonstrating mastery of course content, but by mastering the process itself. They play the game. They follow directions, do the assigned work, ace the tests, get the grades, and graduate. Maybe they become professionals or entrepreneurs. They succeed by the external measures counted in school, but without initiative, inspiration, or self-motivated achievement, and—worst of all—without the thrill of true learning that would sustain them through the next chapters of their lives.

At university and in the workplace, where they have more freedom and less structure, their colleagues and managers wonder: *Why aren't these people better team players? Why do they always seek permission and approval from authority figures? Why don't they take more initiative?*

"The traits that make successful students often stymie performance in the workplace," says Tara Mohr, author of *Playing Big: Practical Wisdom for Women Who Want to Speak Up, Create and Lead.* "Good student behaviors— seeking outside knowledge, pleasing others, and adapting to authority—are the opposite of what you need to be an innovative go-getter."[8]

Dazzlingly bright and successful people come to the university with straight-A transcripts, impressive extracurricular experiences, and sparkling personal recommendations. Entrepreneurs, executives, and professionals rise to the top of their fields and contribute to our civilization's well-being and advancement.

Every one of these all-stars privately confide a variety of sentiments that can be summed up as: *Nothing I did in school prepared me for this.* This is far from personal insecurity or paranoia; even graduate and professional schools are suspect when it comes to preparing students for the world they'll encounter after graduation. Law school was once considered a ticket to the good life, but now, "The fundamental issue is that law schools are producing people who are not capable of being counselors. They are lawyers in the sense that they have law degrees, but they aren't ready to be a provider of services."[9]

If school isn't helping the most talented among us, what is it doing to everyone else?

Today this question has more wide-ranging implications than ever. Every generation has its issues with school, but today's issues—the environment, the economy, our politics, and our culture—call us to pay attention to the matter in a different way. Our approaches to the problems of the world are functions of the way we learn and—ideally—think. The question becomes: *How can we help more people think more effectively?*

As the saying goes, the first step in solving a problem is admitting you have one.

The 2013 report of the Equity & Excellence Commission, a 27-member panel of experts convened by former U.S. Secretary of Education Arne Duncan, begins with these words: "America's K-12 education system, taken as a whole, fails our nation and too many of our children. Our system does not distribute opportunity equitably."[10]

Many of today's students contend with unprecedented levels of trauma, poverty, and associated mental and physical health issues. "More students," according to a 2020 *U.S. News & World Report* assessment of federal data, "are living in emergency shelters, cars, motels, on the street or in some other temporary housing situation than ever before."[11]

It is not realistic to expect school to solve broader societal problems such as poverty, economic inequality, racism, misogyny, or institutionalized violence.

Our system of public education is funded and managed in ways that hurt the students who need the most help. As *The Atlantic*'s Alana Semuels points out, "Districts (in high poverty areas) tend to have more students in need of extra help, and yet they have fewer guidance counselors, tutors, and psychologists, lower-paid teachers, more dilapidated facilities and bigger class sizes than wealthier districts."[12]

The circumstances and the process of school as it is currently administered can turn learning into a daily exercise of tolerating the system. The kindergartner who asks a thousand questions can become the second grader who tires of staring at a workbook—or, more recently, a website—full of math problems. If an inspiring learning opportunity does not present itself, or a caring adult does not actively intervene, the middle school student who lacks the inspiration and motivation gives up and becomes the high school cynic who gazes at a screen all day.

In the end, the result for an entire generation is a system that betrays far too many. Consider: in an age of supposed unprecedented opportunity and possibility, more than 2 million students in one year were listed by the National Center for Education Statistics as "status dropouts" (that is, they were not enrolled in school and had not earned a diploma or equivalency credential).[13] That means, in just one year, the financial and professional futures of a new group the size of a large city were destroyed, along with their hopes of successful, fulfilled lives, and their fundamental belief in a social system's ability to live up to its promise.

Learners need immediate solutions. So, rather than add to the list of criticisms and complaints about school, let's sum up the current state of affairs in two central ideas.

First, the ramifications of school as it currently operates are more deeply rooted and insidious than we account for in our public discussions about education policy. Dropouts and graduates alike are under immense pressure. When you are focused on your physical, mental, emotional, and economic survival, and the constant drumbeat of a message is "graduate in order to get a job and maybe make a little more money than your parents," the idea of learning for learning's sake, rigorous thinking, and any sort of intellectualism starts to look like a luxury for other people.

The pressure of overthinking extends to educators as well, many of whom leave the profession and/or develop a negative regard for the institution of school.

These trends have become so prevalent that they have become woven into the life and career of every American.

The second idea is better news: Anyone can change all of this for themselves and their learning community right now.

This is where Open-Source Learning leaves the well-worn path of school, and leads to the Academy of One.

The Academy of One begins with you. You are the first One. You are the epicenter of your learning. The Academy of One extends to the people you attract to your network beginning with local social systems, including your learning community, your professional community, and your neighborhood.

The Academy of One extends to the virtual communities you create and the networks of interest and support through which you can build bonds with people all over the world.

If enough of us engage in this way, the Academy of One becomes an inclusive, unifying principle that engages people who recognize each other as practicing a philosophy in a functioning global network of learning where all participants can access all the information, support, and critical guidance we need.

You can begin an Academy of One with a single mouse click. You can invite people to join with a network of conversations. You can engage with classmates, an entire school or organization, a community. . . . Together, using models already established in education and on the internet, we can create a global Academy of One and—for the first time in human history—share a universally public system of education.

The limitations of school as we know it are signposts of opportunity. You do not need a teacher or administrator to approve of you creating a blog or a website and inviting others to learn with you. You never needed anyone's approval to be curious, care, ask a question, or search for answers.

If your high school does not teach something you think is important and want to learn—say, how to manage personal finances, prepare tax returns, or organize a funeral—why waste time and energy complaining or petitioning to a bureaucracy when you can begin your Open-Source Learning inquiry right now and immediately add value for yourself and others?

Rather than count on a system to do the things it clearly cannot, we can use Open-Source Learning to step up and support the existing system by doing what Americans have always done: identify a challenge and meet it.

We can augment our formal education with a modified approach to learning because the issues here extend far beyond the fundamental flaws found in compulsory education. We can involve students as full partners in the education experience, demonstrating the excitement of true learning, and appreciating the joy of discovery and encountering new challenges.

There are tangible, practical reasons why Open-Source Learning has relevance in an increasingly digital world. The internet is immune to the school shootings, outbreaks of disease, and natural disasters that close school campuses. Our society and our world are changing faster than our social institutions. Our system of education is designed for constancy and not agility, adaptability, or flexibility. Education is not keeping pace with the exponential acceleration of technology or the digital realm's effects on our lifestyles, our government, and our careers. The result is a formal system of instruction that is supposed to prepare students for their lives and careers, but that instead grows less and less relevant every day.

At this point in history, our ignorance is our peril. What we don't learn about our civic identities, opportunities, or responsibilities increasingly haunts us in a society with increasingly dominant narratives of inequality and adversarial politics.

The world off-campus threatens to invalidate the social contract of school. It is no longer ethical, or even truthful, to promise young people that education and graduation will guarantee them better lives than their parents.

People are indicating less confidence in the value of higher education. In the past, Americans attended colleges and universities to prepare for careers that were already well-established. When today's high school freshmen graduate from college eight years from now, many will work in jobs that don't yet exist. Yet, only about half of U.S. adults (51 percent) now consider a college education to be "very important," down from 70 percent in 2013.[14]

In any organizational system, we want the confidence of knowing that the boss knows what to do. But many students believe that they know more about modern life and technology than their teachers. From the school site to the top echelon of government, the troops too often take little inspiration or direction from those in positions of authority.

Media theorist Douglas Rushkoff observes that teachers' authority is no longer derived the same way: "Teachers used to base their authority on their exclusive access to the information their students wished to learn. Now that students can find nearly all the information they need online, the role of a teacher must change to that of a guide or coach—more of a partner in learning who helps students evaluate and synthesize the data they find."[15]

Many teachers have not been able or willing to make this sort of adjustment. This has eroded the amount of respect they receive. Citing a Harris Poll, Julia Ryan of *The Atlantic* observed, "While 79 percent of Americans said students respected teachers when they were in school, only 31 percent believe students respect teachers today."[16]

These factors intensify the trauma that students face in their daily lives. Talk to any teacher or student and they will tell you what's wrong with school, what's missing, what's important to them, and—most especially— why they think nothing is ever going to change.

As anyone who has successfully navigated a toxic relationship will tell you, it is far more productive to work on improving yourself than to expect change from the other person. This perspective is especially true when it comes to expecting change in the American system of education, a structure that has weathered tidal waves of criticism, literally for centuries—yet the basic system remains essentially intact since Massachusetts made education the responsibility of society by passing the Old Deluder Satan Act in 1647.[17]

Through Open-Source Learning, we have the opportunity to create profound change in our own *education* in ways that create value, interdependence, and hope through *learning*, and may yet illuminate a path forward for schools.

OPEN-SOURCE LEARNING:
THE POWER TO TRANSFORM

Professional educators and advisors understand that

a) no matter how well we think we understand the institution of education, we can change ourselves and our habits far more easily than we can change school;

b) we have far more thinking and computing power than we realize, and certainly more than we need to create better lives for ourselves and our communities through learning;

c) because we now have the internet, and several decades of online experience to draw on, and we can adopt meaningful practices that will help transform learning and create benefits for everyone involved . . .

d) . . . and we can do so without spending a single extra dollar.

The tools for the task are so formidable that they would have been inconceivable only a few decades ago. A single average smartphone today has more processing power than all of the computers at NASA that guided the Apollo missions to the moon. According to one analysis, "Put simply, the iPhone 6's clock is 32,600 times faster than the best Apollo era computers and could perform instructions 120,000,000 times faster. You wouldn't be wrong in saying an iPhone could be used to guide 120,000,000 Apollo era spacecraft to the moon, all at the same time."[18]

The vast trove of basic facts that we once had to learn in school are now a click away online.

We still need education—just not the kind for which school as we know it was built 400 years ago.

THE EMERGENCE OF OPEN-SOURCE LEARNING

Many teachers peek over the walls of learning management systems and password-protected portfolios to use the public internet as a delivery system for coursework. Some teachers create course blogs to save paper and create a platform that gave absent students a way to keep up. A few teachers realize that online components of a course introduce possibilities that extend far beyond school.

There is so much we can do to connect classroom learning with real life and what students wanted to know.

The education system may attempt to constrain the capabilities of digital technology, but the potential for these resources should be obvious: advances in microprocessor speed and bandwidth have totally changed the game.

In the 1980s, users waited for a modem to shriek its snail-pace connection; now, a single click instantly unlocks libraries of information. Educators and learners can share digital tools of their own creation and collaborate face-to-face online with anyone on Earth. Create. Remix. Distribute knowledge on a global scale. The possibilities are endless.

In many ways, Open-Source Learning follows in the footsteps of Waldorf, Montessori, Reggio-Emilia, and even Plato's Academy, in that it is self-directed, student-centered, and interdisciplinary. However, Open-Source Learning differs from all of these, as well as contemporary "open education" and "open education resources" in one important respect—every member of an Open-Source Learning network can clone and fork the curriculum, the processes, and even the tools used for instruction and curation. And they can use the internet to do it.

* * *

I began using the term "Open-Source Learning" to describe my approach to teaching in 2006, shortly after I moved from Los Angeles to California's Central Coast, about halfway between San Francisco and Los Angeles. As word got around that I was doing something different in the classroom, I needed a way to describe my practice of teaching to parents, teachers, and school administrators in a region best known for barbecue.

It may be hard to believe now, but in the early 2000s many schools didn't allow students anywhere near the public internet; going online was considered dangerous: adults feared "stranger danger," the possibility that students would be exposed to vices like porn or gambling, or—worse—that students would say or do things that would embarrass the teacher or the school.

My approach to teaching was considered so unusual that my students were featured on radio and television. Journalists sought me out for interviews. First they asked about my methods. Then they asked if I expected to be fired.

The origins of the term "Open-Source Learning" comes from systems theory. Debora Hammond, Peter Senge, and others have used systems theory as a compelling way to describe interactions and qualities of communication and relationships in families, schools, organizations, societies, and the natural world.

The most important implications of "open systems" and "closed systems" for schools have to do with the ways open systems can amplify and accelerate learning by responding to and interacting with the surrounding environment. An open system network can change its structure and purpose in ways that enhance the quality of the information that is being shared and absorbed in that system (more on this in chapter 3). Closed systems, such as classrooms, are limited and do not benefit from what is happening in the outside world.

The perfect example of how systems change is how we learn. Every time you meet someone new and exchange ideas, you're not only enriching each other, you're creating new neuronal connections—literally, changing your mind—and creating opportunities for others to do the same. In other words, you're learning and teaching.

In a school, students working together can create exponential growth for learning by collaborating online, reaching out to experts, and building small networks that could support and critique their work.

The appeal of Open-Source Learning first gained attention in Silicon Valley. In 2011, the Institute for the Future, a Palo Alto think tank near Stanford University, selected "The Open-Source School" as a "Vision for

California's Future." The Institute brought leading innovators together to discuss the idea. Over time, Open-Source Learning has been refined and distilled into the ideas we will explore together here.

* * *

What is Open-Source Learning?

1. Learners take charge of their own learning.

From the first day of an Open-Source Learning experience, students are full partners in developing their own educational missions, plans, and decision-making.

In the Open-Source Learning classroom, the teacher's role shifts substantially. Apart from administrative responsibilities that continue unchanged, the teacher becomes much less of a lecturer and much more of a facilitator, mentoring students as they develop their critical thinking and articulate the reasons for developing their course of inquiry. The teacher also guides students in becoming members of a network that develops and appraises their work.

2. Open-Source Learning network members create and manage digital records of their learning journeys.

Students create tangible, reproduceable material that documents their learning experiences, which become part of their global digital record and available to everyone. Coursework and individual learning journeys are transparent, integral elements of the educational experience. Network members establish online identities. They connect with peers and mentors around the world that create additional networks, communities of support, and critique.

3. Anyone can clone and create new content and processes.

In the same way as coders use open-source software development repositories, teachers and students who practice Open-Source Learning can copy, remix, and use ideas to develop their own material, in real life and on the internet.

Students learn about fair use and Creative Commons licenses. They learn to share their work as well as the contributions of their teachers and mentors. They remix content, processes, and tools in ways that meet their needs.

It is important to remember that "digital natives" are not "digital experts." Students may spend an inordinate amount of time staring at their phones, but they may not understand the structural technology of the internet, its business models, how it is used to share their data, or its influence on our economy, our government, our culture, or our thinking.

High school and college graduates (and their parents and teachers) need to connect and learn more about concepts such as intellectual property, adversarial inoperability, dark patterns, search algorithms, filter bubbles, and other concepts that have an ongoing influence on our society and the choices we make every day.

Open-Source Learning has become a philosophy of education built around a guided learning process that combines timeless best practices with today's tools in a way that empowers learners of any age, in school or elsewhere, to create paths of inquiry, communities of interest and critique, and a portfolio of knowledge that is part of the global digital record—all skills that are directly transferable to the job market.

Open-Source Learning works differently than any other education movement in history, for one simple reason: we have the internet. This does *not* refer to the routine use of the internet to find entertainment or information, as we have all been doing since the 1990s. Rather, it means capitalizing on the extraordinary power of digital technology to enlighten, to inspire, and to connect people in ways that empower their learning beyond any medium ever available before.

Understanding the belief systems that power the internet and influence our society, integrating school with life off-campus, and exploring technology to learn in new and inspiring ways helps us all develop our ability to find, analyze, evaluate, synthesize, and share resources that amplify and accelerate learning in every domain. Offering learners these opportunities seems like basic, timeless best practice in teaching. But common sense, that sense we share in common, is a precious and rapidly vanishing commodity in today's world. The next generation of learners is depending on us to protect creativity, curiosity, and trust in the context of today's standardized schooling systems so that transparency and collaboration become normal, and Open-Source Learning practices are no longer seen as extraordinary, much less magic.

Chapter 2

Do You Believe in Magic?

The best works are often those with the fewest and simplest elements
. . . until you look at them a little more, and things start to happen.

Clifford Still, in *Abstract Expressionism*[1]

When we are no longer able to change a situation, we are challenged
to change ourselves.

Viktor Frankl, *Man's Search for Meaning*[2]

Thirty-five of his classmates sat at their desks, slack-jawed and staring at
Pablo Cruz.[3] As the shock wore off, everyone started talking at once:

"Whoa! Dude! Did you see that? What the . . .?"

A warm afternoon in late May is not exactly prime time for capturing the
attention of high school juniors, but in that moment, Pablo owned the room
and everyone in it. He stood at the front and smiled.

Pablo had spent the most of the year researching how magic depends on
perception, attention, and focus. The fact that he was teaching class as a student was not unique—all of his classmates were also teaching, based on what
they'd learned about their Big Questions, in the annual Open-Source Learning
"Masterpiece Academy"—but Pablo's learning journey led him to a particularly deep conceptual understanding and a demonstrably high level of skill.
Pablo, in this moment, was truly the student who had become the master.

He started inauspiciously, with a garden variety "pick a card, any card" trick
that impressed exactly no one. Students yawned and looked at their phones.
Pablo ignored their disinterest like a veteran performer in a dinner theater.

The illusions became more unpredictable as the show went on. After a variation on three-card monte with a double lift, Pablo asked a student to write her name on a card. He ripped up the card and asked another student across the room to reach down into her backpack and open the sealed envelope inside. She opened the envelope, gasped, and held up the signed card, which was now taped and in one piece.

The room grew quiet. Brows furrowed.

Then, the grand finale. At some point along the way, right there in front of everyone, Pablo had changed the t-shirt he was wearing. When he started, his t-shirt was black; by the end, he had somehow changed it to a red one—without taking off the button-down shirt or the jacket he was wearing over it. No one noticed this until he pointed it out at the end of his performance.

Everyone went bananas as their brains frantically tried to catch up with what they had just seen.

"I know," Pablo said, "Magic is like that. You think you're paying attention to something, and then you realize that you're really not getting the whole picture. Your mind talks you into believing what you're seeing.

"It's like when you're walking on stairs in the dark, and you think there's another stair. But you take the step and there's nothing there; your foot finds only empty space, or the floor jumps up and trips you.

"Either way, now you're out of balance and you have to deal with two realities: one is the reality that is actually out there, and has been there the whole time. The other reality is what happens when you try to take the step that isn't there—you have to face the fact that you didn't know. You have to admit to yourself that you were acting on what you believed to be true, which was wrong, because actually you had no idea what was right in front of you the whole time."

To illustrate his point, Pablo showed a video from a research study done by psychologists Dan Simons and Christopher Chabris. Before Pablo started the video, he told students that they would be watching people passing a basketball, and he asked everyone to count the number of passes. What Pablo did not mention—and the majority of the audience did not see until he rewound the video and played it in slow motion to prove that it actually happened—was the person in the gorilla suit who walked right through the basketball game.

This was a common finding in the original research study; Simons and Chabris call the phenomenon *selective attention*. Simons and Chabris evaluated many similar studies and experiences and concluded that our strategies for processing information "Reveal an important truth: our minds don't work the way we think they do. We think we see ourselves and the world as they really are, but we're actually missing a whole lot."[4]

It is great fun for a magician like Pablo to manipulate our attention and then "reveal" reality to us as it has actually existed all along, but it makes you wonder: *What are we missing the rest of the time?*

When it comes to the way we think—and specifically the way we think about school—we are missing quite a lot of information. Attending school does not generally involve investigating our own mental capabilities in this way. School also does not invite close scrutiny or encourage constructively critical public discussion of this fact.

As a result, this sort of critical thinking is not baked into our culture, and most discussions about school, education, and learning are like Pablo's description of that last step in the dark. We practice selective attention without even knowing it. Our perceptions inform our thinking, but our perceptions leave out a lot of information, and all the while we are not even aware that we are missing anything.

Being aware of limitations in what we perceive and understand is half the battle. David Foster Wallace illustrated the point with an old story in a commencement speech at Kenyon College: "There are these two young fish swimming along and they happen to meet an older fish swimming the other way, who nods at them and says, 'Morning, boys. How's the water?' The two young fish swim on for a bit, and eventually one of them looks over at the other and goes, 'What the hell is water?'"[5]

In the absence of complete, accurate information about school as it actually functions, we are guided by our beliefs about what we think school is and does. As Alfie Kohn, an advocate for progressive education, wrote in *The Washington Post*, "A certain ideology, along with a set of empirical assumptions, underlies most conversations about education in this country, most of what actually happens in schools, and most proposals for change."[6]

Even inside schools it's hard to stop and think. The fast pace of school calendars, the seemingly endless tasks, and the culture of school administration leaves little room for teachers and students to engage in deep thought or substantive conversations about the underlying belief system of education. So, before introducing the models and practices associated with Open-Source Learning, we need some context about how we think about the water in which educators and learners swim.

ABSTRACT EXPRESSIONISM

Expressing ourselves is one thing; making ourselves understood is altogether different, especially when we exchange ideas about belief systems.

The challenge of understanding and sharing the meanings of abstract ideas is not unique to psychology, philosophy, or the operational politics and logistics of school. For instance, learning the fundamentals of algebra is a similarly tough leap because it takes a learner from the familiar experience of arithmetic—where whole, rational numbers can be represented by tangible objects in the world—to the realm of representational mathematics, where symbols stand for sets of numbers.

Sets of numbers are collections of multiple things, but they are also considered things by themselves, regardless of how many other things they contain, which also makes them ideas, which is enough to give anyone a headache unless they can somehow simplify or visualize the conversation.

Because clarifying and sharing the meanings of abstractions is so hard, especially in a fast-moving culture in which "TL;DR" (Too Long; Didn't Read) has become a Thing, we have adopted shorthand strategies for the purpose.

All of our learning deals in symbols—at this very moment you are interpreting symbols on a page or a screen as you read this.

Open-Source Learning expands our understanding of symbols, which may include figurative language, numbers, corporate logos, or even emojis, by explicitly bringing them into the conversation to where everyone can see and analyze them.

Symbols that stand for ideas are essential to our understanding concepts that do not actually exist in the physical world. Symbols are efficient. This is important because our brains estimate potential values and rewards to figure how much cognitive effort we should invest—and decide to work harder or give up—without our knowledge. Exactly how we do this is a mystery.

Neuroscientists have investigated this process by using fMRI and concluded, "the neural mechanisms for expectation processes under conditions of incomplete information are unknown."[7] We don't know exactly what will entice a learner to invest the brainpower needed to really understand an abstract idea.

Because most schools and individuals don't engage in training that builds our capacity to process abstractions, educators are constantly racing against the "I just don't get it" moment that can frustrate a learner and make them give up. We choose the fastest, easiest ways to get our message across.

Entire digital systems of communication rely on the same principle. Why explain complicated concepts in multiple paragraphs when you can click on an emoji?

Thoughtful people have spent lifetimes trying to understand the concept of happiness, and we still strip our mental gears just trying to pick the right words to define and explain the idea. On the other hand, if you show anyone a yellow circle with two dots and a smile—or even this simple symbol :)—they can tell you exactly what it signifies in less than a second. The same thing applies with a heart and the concept of love, or to a religious symbol, such as a crucifix or the Star of David, and the concept of God.

The practice of representing an abstract concept with a tangible, concrete symbol is called *reification*. Computer science, statistics, and logic all depend on reification to engage people in a symbolic story that is easy to understand.

We haven't quite figured out how to reify learning. We know that learning exists, and we can symbolize a moment of connection or understanding with a lightbulb or an "Aha!" But what happens in the learning process is extremely personal, and very messy. All of those neatly organized school curriculums and classroom lesson plans are artificial superimpositions on a nonlinear mystery.

Learning isn't necessarily connected in time or behavior with specific content, objects, or actions. If you have ever thought of just the right thing to say—hours after the conversation ended, maybe as you woke up from a nap—you know the feeling. Our minds are constantly reflecting, solving problems, and discovering better ways to do things, even in our sleep. But, it is really hard to demonstrate and explain these internal processes in ways others can understand, much less in those few minutes before the class bell rings.

How can we represent our learning, or the concept of learning itself? Can learning be effectively represented by test scores, grades, the number of words in an essay, or anything else we can measure? Can we infer substantive meaning about a person's mental presence or absence from their attendance record?

We should take care in how we represent learning, and we should question whether to believe what we see. Sometimes reification oversimplifies an idea or even shifts the emphasis from one idea to another. Money was originally invented as a way of communicating about the value of other things. It was a symbol without any intrinsic meaning of its own. However, over time, belief systems about money evolved, and some of those beliefs contributed to a shift away from money as currency and toward money as a desirable end in and of itself. The same can be said about grades and test scores.

This is troubling when it comes to our belief systems about education. If we don't acknowledge the role our beliefs play in limiting our perspectives, we may never understand each other, or this moment in the history of humanity, schooling, and learning.

THE POWER OF BELIEFS

Our belief systems are so deeply ingrained in us that they not only influence the way we see the world, but they also give us a sense of who we are and how we relate to others.

The specific beliefs we hold are secondary—we can always change those if we want to—but the fact that we *believe* is hardwired. It is one of the defining characteristics that make us human in the first place. You can (sometimes) take a person out of a particular belief system, but you cannot take the system of believing out of a person.

Learning is essentially an updating of our belief systems as we encounter new information. The process enables us to adapt and thrive in the changing world around us. Understanding why we think the way we think helps us recognize opportunities for improvement.

Around 70,000 years ago, *Homo sapiens* beat out the Neanderthals, Denisovans, and other hominids to became the dominant species on Earth and start the Cognitive Revolution. Our superpower was not the use of fire or development of language—lots of other animals use language. What made us different is that we use our language to tell a special kind of story: fiction.

Human beings create stories full of imaginary ideas—abstractions that convey values, concepts, and rituals about ourselves and our world.

When other people recognize these stories and their symbols, our shared imaginary ideas become big enough to unite us in large numbers that transcend individual differences, geographic boundaries, and even languages. They give us a sense of belonging and purpose, and they galvanize us to do things together that we couldn't possibly do alone.

Our ability to connect and collaborate through the use of imaginary things—the power we derive from the beliefs we share in invisible, common myths—is what distinguishes *Homo sapiens* from every other species. We can communicate, organize, and coordinate activities in large numbers based on symbols for ideas that exist nowhere in nature other than in our minds.

These stories become important to us. We identify with these myths, legends, gods, and monsters. Religion is one example among many others: political parties, countries, college football teams, every "ism" you can imagine. These self-identifications have a great deal of influence on our relationships, our purchasing habits, and the lessons we teach our children.

We honor the stories' authority over the way things are in the world, and we behave in ways that identify us as members of a particular story's tribe. It's the only explanation for an otherwise mature adult celebrating or grieving the result of a game played by strangers thousands of miles away.

As Yuval Noah Harari wrote in *Sapiens*, "Ever since the Cognitive Revolution, Sapiens have thus been living in a dual reality. On the one hand, the objective reality of rivers, trees and lions; and on the other hand, the imagined reality of gods, nations and corporations. As time went by, the imagined reality became ever more powerful, so that today the very survival of rivers, trees and lions depends on the grace of imagined entities such as the United States and Google."[8]

The narratives can become dominant—godlike, even—especially when we don't question them or engage with them critically.

A story about the value of money can evolve into a shared social system like capitalism that dominates the global economy. A story about how digital technology will make everything better can become education policy that institutionalizes the practice of staring at screens, even as it works against our self-interest through the mass adoption of smartphones and home appliances that keep us all distracted and under constant surveillance.

The power of our belief in narratives helps explain a modern culture in which entities that only exist in our minds (such as political parties, religions, the United States of America, Facebook) have such enormous influence over the objective, factually verifiable, physical world we experience with our senses (the air we breathe, the water we drink, the portion of our paycheck we get to keep).

Countries, governments, sports teams, religions, corporations—all of these are invented ideas that exist only in our agreements about meaning.

So is the institution of education.

School is just a product of our collective imagination.

Over time, beliefs about the purpose, structure, and operation of school in America have created a culture that has endured for generations, complete with rituals, sins, and sacraments: the way in which students line up and sit, the way teachers call roll and use the word "tardy"—all of these are functions of a very specific shared culture.

In 1647, Massachusetts passed the Old Deluder Satan Act, creating compulsory education in America by requiring communities with more than 50 families to appoint and pay a teacher, and communities with more than 100 families to establish a grammar school. The general idea at the time was not to provide a well-rounded education, but rather to ensure that everyone could read scripture, and thus avoid being fooled by Satan.

In the 370-plus years between the passing of that law and the writing of this sentence, there has never once been a time in which everyone in any American community raised their voices in unison to celebrate the institution of school as perfect, or even excellent, in meeting the needs of every student.

In some education policy and research circles, the history of education is also described as the history of education reform. That history is full of criticism and complaint.

Today's commentary on school continues the tradition: it seems like every week brings a new story about problems in schools: violence, inappropriate use of technology, attempts to ban "subversive" books, standardized testing, sexual misconduct, physical abuse, substance abuse, mistreatment of students with special needs . . . the list goes on and on.

Nevertheless, the essential structure and culture of school—the stories we tell ourselves about school—remain intact. Changes in laws and policies have not changed outcomes for students.

Teachers are trained and compelled to uphold the belief system of school. They are required to teach state-approved curriculum and to "manage" their classrooms according to expected norms.

This means that teachers often find themselves in the uncomfortable position of having to ignore real-world information—for instance, that thirty-seven students in a class have wildly different life experiences, traumas, goals, emotions, brain chemistry, and learning capacities—in order to maintain the belief system ("today we are all going to learn photosynthesis").

One element of this belief system holds that the teacher must discipline students in an effort to minimize every form of distraction, so many teachers actively deter students from using their phones in class.

As a result, when students in these classes encounter a word or concept they do not understand, they do not take out their phones. They actively practice not being curious.

Not being curious is the enemy of learning. School policies that deter research are strange. Young people not looking at their phones when they need information is especially strange, when Americans look at their phones *more than 8 billion times a day.*[9] Open-Source Learning encourages students to learn to harness the power of their devices as research and productivity tools.

By acknowledging reality, instead of imposing a fiction on people that demands they ignore what is right in front of them, Open-Source Learning makes it easier for learners to focus on learning, instead of protecting themselves against being gaslighted.

The need to connect with our own sources of curiosity, the value of knowledge, and each other is shared by people of every background, socioeconomic status, race, religion, gender, and political party.

History tells us that school as an institution is not going to transform itself, but it is only an institution because it's supported by our individual and social beliefs, and those we can change.

BELIEFS ABOUT LEARNING

Learning is often attributed to factors outside the learner: an excellent teacher, a meaningful experience, a well-planned lesson or curriculum, or a high production value instructional resource.

Although learners may respond positively to any or all of these, the true source of learning resides inside each of us. We are born learning, that is, actively interacting with our environment to figure out our world, our place in it, and even ourselves.

Maybe that's why we like learning so much better than we like school. Learning is what makes us human and connects us. School often treats us like things and isolates us.

As a high school student wrote: "Students love learning, we just hate to be taught."[10]

Unfortunately, student feedback doesn't usually find its way into policy debates or school reform. When journalists write about the challenges facing K-12 schools, they usually ask university professors or administrators about the issues. Students and teachers don't have much influence when it comes to how school operates. They don't hold the purse strings, they are not considered experts, and they are not consulted for their views on making substantive changes.

Managers and educators often design systems and "learning experiences" based on state curriculum standards and hierarchical authority, without fully understanding the learner's experience. When it comes to their schooling, students experience little empathy.

In 2019, a summer school class of incoming high school freshmen explored the difference between sympathy and empathy. Vivecca answered this way:

"Sympathy," she said, "is when you feel sorry for someone else, and empathy is when you let them know that you understand and identify with their feelings or their experience."

Empathy is vital to the success of any teacher, in any setting. As the popular saying goes, "People don't care how much you know until they know how much you care."

There are obvious and necessary gaps in perspective between teacher and student. The teacher is often a different race, ethnicity, sex, gender, and socio-economic status than the students. The teacher is always years older than the students, and must rely on memory and empathy in order to connect with the students and their lived experiences.

In addition, many K-12 students are dealing with levels of trauma that adults can't possibly understand from their pre-pandemic, pre-9/11, pre-internet and social media, pre-surveillance technology, pre-school shootings, pre-(whatever we're calling this political moment) experience.

For example, consider these exchanges between high school juniors and a middle-aged, white teacher, all of which occurred *within one hour*:

Guadalupe arrived late for class.

"The cops were out," she said.

"At your house? Is everything OK?"

"Oh yeah, they weren't at my house. They were down the block. But my mom doesn't have papers so we couldn't go out until they left."

Jesus stared at his phone. His eyes were red and welling up with tears.

"What's up?"

Jesus held up a picture. "That's my dad. He rolled a stop sign two months ago. But when the police pulled him over, they weren't traffic cops. They were ICE. They took him somewhere and we haven't seen him since."

Michael came to the room at lunch to make up a final exam.

"Why weren't you in class for the test?"

"Someone shot my brother in the face at the laundromat last night."

Not every teacher deals with the same issues, but everyone who has stood in front of a classroom has had moments when the concerns of the student transcend their own life experiences. An educator does not need to memorize Abraham Maslow's "Hierarchy of Needs" to understand that if we don't feel safe or secure, we are not going to learn very well or get close to fulfilling our potential.

School was not designed to provide multiple channels for expression and direct feedback so that the teacher and the students can better understand each other and meet each other's learning needs. As many scholars and pundits have observed, our model of school resembles an Industrial Age factory, where processes are optimized for efficiency and outcomes are quantified.

Ken Robinson, whose TED talk on schools[11] resonated so strongly that it has been viewed more than 65 million times online, wrote, "Public schools were not only created in the interests of industrialism—they were created in the image of industrialism. In many ways, they reflect the factory culture they were designed to support.

"This is especially true in high schools," Robinson wrote, "where school systems base education on the principles of the assembly line and the efficient division of labor." Schools divide the curriculum into specialist segments: some teachers install math in the students, and others install history. They arrange the day into standard units of time, marked out by the ringing of bells, much like a factory announcing the beginning of the workday and the end of breaks.

"Students are educated in batches, according to age, as if the most important thing they have in common is their date of manufacture. They are given standardized tests at set points and compared with each other before being sent out onto the market."[12]

In order to get beyond the commodification of curriculum as "rigor" and students as "graduation rates," we have to delve into what makes learning most rewarding, and also messy: its humanity.

We have to create a culture of empathy for ourselves.

THE CALL TO ADVENTURE

The power of ritual and belief is also important in terms of the learner's place in society. School and graduation are time-honored rites of passage in American culture. Generations of Americans have taught their children that graduating high school is the signal of discipline, knowledge, and readiness to take a seat at the adults' table, and that a diploma is a ticket to a better life.

Over the last several decades, however, fewer and fewer Americans believe in our social institutions, including school. According to the latest Gallup "Confidence in Institutions" poll, 29 percent of American adults have "a great deal/quite a lot" of confidence in public schools—and 29 percent of American adults have "very little/none."[13]

Fractures in our shared beliefs are creating a crisis of trust. In the Information Age, we receive so much content through so many channels from so many sources for so many reasons that people don't know what or whom to believe. There is increasing suspicion of politicians, experts, and the media. Even words like "facts" and "truth" have become subjects for debate. Facts that were once considered obvious, and truths that were once considered self-evident, are now ignored or (mis)characterized as controversial whenever a person or a group decides that those facts or truths are in conflict with a particular opinion or worldview.

Evolution, vaccination, and the that fact that climate change is a manmade effect are not, in point of fact, controversial, or even debatable on the merits of verifiable evidence, any more than is the law of gravity (which, if you are truly super-enthusiastic about challenging the idea, you may test, by stepping off the edge of a really tall building. Once).

The confusion and resulting tension created by all of this is straining traditional beliefs about school to the breaking point.

Psychologist Leon Festinger coined a term for what happens when a person tries to hold contradictory beliefs simultaneously: "cognitive dissonance." To a point, cognitive dissonance can be productive because it creates a powerful impulse to understand and resolve the conflict—the students watching Pablo perform magic developed an intense curiosity, a motivation to figure out exactly what was going on.

In fact, the first hypothesis that Festinger wrote was, "The existence of dissonance, being psychologically uncomfortable, will motivate the person to try to relieve dissonance and achieve consonance."[14]

However, when the issue seems too big to handle, or the game seems to be rigged against you whether you understand it or not (like the widening gap between what school provides and what learners need in the world), cognitive dissonance creates a great deal of confusion and stress.

One way to reduce the effects of cognitive dissonance is to ignore or resist any new information that challenges how our existing beliefs lead us to think and act. In 2012, the Texas State Board of Education made this statement its official policy platform: "We oppose the teaching of . . . critical thinking skills and similar programs . . . which focus on behavior modification and have the purpose of challenging the student's fixed beliefs."[15]

The problem, of course, is that blind allegiance to our preexisting beliefs prevents us from learning or doing anything new. And assuming there is a last stair in the dark can cause us to fall on our faces.

THE ACE UP OUR SLEEVE

We do have another choice. We can choose to see our circumstances as an invitation to learn in a different way. Marcus Aurelius, the emperor of Rome whose "Meditations" are often quoted as examples of Stoic philosophy, put it this way: "Our actions may be impeded . . . but there can be no impeding our intentions or dispositions. Because we can accommodate and adapt."[16]

For students who have never had the opportunity to learn how to adapt and are simply doing their best to work through a difficult process without getting in trouble, it can be hard to discover and stay true to our intentions or dispositions.

Open-Source Learning treats this as an opportunity: a call to adventure.

Joseph Campbell described the call to adventure in his study of the hero's journey—also known as the monomyth, the story archetype shared by cultures around the world throughout history. Campbell pointed out that we are often called to adventure through a misstep or an undesirable set of circumstances.

As Campbell wrote in *The Hero with a Thousand Faces*,

> A blunder—apparently the merest chance—reveals an unsuspected world, and the individual is drawn into a relationship with forces that are not rightly understood. . . . But whether small or great, and no matter what stage or grade in life, the call rings up the curtain, always, on a mystery of transfiguration—a rite, or moment, of spiritual passage, which, when complete, amounts to a dying and a birth. The familiar life horizon has been outgrown; the old concepts, ideals, and emotional patterns no longer fit; the time for the passing of a threshold is at hand.[17]

While we may wish that things in school and society were different, it is easier to change our own minds than to persuade others or shift entire institutions. And the better we get at changing our minds based on accurate information, the more we will improve our quality of life.

Many would-be heroes refuse the call to adventure, electing instead to stay with what's familiar, no matter how undesirable that future may be. One teacher recently described her fear about replacing a principal: "Oh, she is horrible—but you never know, the next person could be worse. Sometimes the devil you know is better than the devil you don't."

We are driven by the monomyth; some of the most well-known stories of our culture follow its formula. *Star Wars* creator George Lucas has cited Joseph Campbell's work as a major influence, especially in creating the motivation—or hesitation—of his key characters. In the first *Star Wars* movie, Luke Skywalker does not respond positively when Obi-Wan Kenobi first invites Luke to leave home and join the rebellion. You would think Luke would jump at the chance—this is what he has wanted all along. But he hems and haws, saying he has responsibilities at home. It is not until Luke goes home, and finds his house burned and his family killed, that he answers the call to adventure.

How bad must things get before we decide to explore the unknown in search of something better?

Many high school students have experiences similar to Luke's. They have dreams, but they refuse the call to adventure because they adopt belief systems about "real world" obligations. They need to make money. They want to help their families.

The examples are everywhere. Consider Joaquin, who could not answer the call because after school he helped his brothers tend crops in the fields, and by the time he got home he was too tired to study. Or Alicia, who earned a full athletic scholarship to the University of Chicago but was reluctant to leave home because her mother was sick. Or Jennifer, who could not hear herself think in her own room because of the arguments between her brother and their parents, but who also could not bring herself to move out because she was afraid that if she left no one would break up the fights.

Even without the extenuating circumstances, by the time many students get to high school, they don't want anything new to upset whatever delicate balance they've created for themselves—they're reluctant to raise their hands in class, much less join a rebellion.

Young people may not know where to go, but, if they are to improve their lives and take their place in our society, they also can't stay where they are.

Open-Source Learning focuses on helping learners and educators choose how we respond to our circumstances. We can view the difficulties that today's students encounter as indicators of unmet needs. Now we have the opportunity to meet those needs.

For example: If everything was terrific, and we weren't missing steps and tripping in the dark, there would be no need to reconsider what and how we learn, and this would be a very short book.

The people who fund and lead schools are not going to fix it on their own. They are the keepers of the stories that made them successful in the first place. It stands to reason that the rich and powerful—or anyone who benefited from the status quo—have always had a vested interest in maintaining the status quo. After all, it worked for them.

Teaching and learning, on the other hand, is the art of fostering new belief systems and charting new courses. On those occasions when new belief systems appear to challenge the existing social order, they can be regarded as threats.

Some of the greatest teachers in history suffered lousy career endings:

- Lao Tzu was so disgusted by the indifference of leaders and the suffering of the people that he just walked off toward the western frontier. If it wasn't for the guard who stopped him and begged him to write down his notes, we wouldn't have the *Tao*.

- Confucius also didn't fit in with unethical leaders. He resigned and spent his later years in exile.
- Socrates was accused by the Athenian government of failing to honor the old gods and of corrupting the youth by introducing new deities. The man who taught Plato and indirectly influenced the course of Western civilization was sentenced to death.

Just in the last few decades, high-profile, successful American educators like John Taylor Gatto and Jaime Escalante achieved extraordinary results with their students, only to be sabotaged and punished for their work by administrators who reinforced the very system that was holding learners back in the first place.

This pattern has not dissuaded many from believing in the story that schooling can fix things. In his book *Capital*, Thomas Piketty points to education as the economic catalyst for social change.

"Historical experience suggests that the principal mechanism for convergence at the international as well as the domestic level is the diffusion of knowledge," Piketty wrote. "In other words, the poor catch up with the rich to the extent that they achieve the same level of technological know-how, skill, and education—not by becoming the property of the wealthy."[18]

According to the National Center for Education Statistics,[19] our nation is investing in education, and graduation rates are improving: in 2017–2018, the United States spent approximately $1.4 trillion for public and private school education, from prekindergarten through graduate school. And over the past four decades, the dropout rate has steadily decreased.

However, economic investment in education and a higher graduation rate is not leveling the economic playing field in America.

Over the same period of time, student loan debt in America has grown to nearly $1.6 trillion,[20] and the gap between the richest and poorest households in America has grown to the largest it has been in the last fifty years.[21]

Whatever learners are getting from school, it is not helping them create value in the marketplace or reduce income inequality.

The old ways are not working. This is where educators and learners may hear a call to adventure—and they must decide for themselves how they will respond. School is not going to fix anything. We are.

THE "LIMINAL" SPACE

When a teacher breaks ranks and does something original, or a person starts a new phase of life, or a school breaks away from Common Core or standard-based testing or any other policy or tradition, it creates a "happy problem."

How do we talk about something that is not "the same ol', same ol'," but is also not standard practice yet because it is being created through the very act of doing it?

It's relatively easy to complain and cast out the old dysfunctional gods of school—lots of people think school could and should be better. But what exactly are the new gods? What are the principles that should guide that improvement?

The truth is, no one knows. The new story of school has not yet been written. We are in between the world that used to be and the world we need to create for learners.

This limbo or "in between" stages of growth, is what it means to be in a liminal state. Understanding that our learners and our society are in liminal states can provide more room for the patience, flexibility, and creativity everyone needs to invent what comes next.

Arthur van Gannep, who coined the phrase "rites of passage" to describe the rituals through which we transition to different stages in life, also invented a word to describe the state we're in when we're in between stages: "liminality."

In van Gannep's words, "I propose to call the rites of separation from the previous world, 'preliminal rites,' those executed during the transitional stage, 'liminal rites,' and the ceremonies of incorporation into the new world 'post-liminal rites.'"[22]

Mythology contains many examples of liminality. When Oedipus encounters the Sphinx on his way to Thebes, he is both a citizen and a stranger. The Sphinx is of this world but also not, and both protector and killer. When Oedipus answers the riddle, he effectively ends one era and begins another.

In the 1960s, Victor Turner extended van Gannep's concept from individual rites of passage with specific rituals to societies moving through formative periods of uncertainty. Turner describes the lack of clarity we experience when we pass a threshold from one state to another: "During the intervening 'liminal' period, the characteristics of the ritual subject are ambiguous; he passes through a cultural realm that has few or none of the attributes of the past or coming state."[23]

Think of the adolescent who lives with one awareness in childhood and another in adulthood—in a sense, the young person's sense of self-identity is no longer based on the past, and it cannot anticipate the future even as it becomes something new. This is the "in between" of metamorphosis. The caterpillar is no longer a caterpillar, but it's not yet a butterfly.

What does all of this mean for educators and learners in school? Or our society as a whole? And what does it have to do with Open-Source Learning?

Open-Source Learning provides a way for us to collaborate around basic principles in ways that invite students and educators alike to investigate their previously held beliefs and create something new, acknowledging all the while that they are in a state of becoming.

Working with what is, as opposed to what we believe should be, enables us to build an intellectual garden for learning and create optimal conditions for growth without attempting to mandate the color and height of the flowers. We can operate according to high standards without forcing everyone to be standardized.

Whatever we do next will inform our ideas of ourselves and what is possible. When Hamlet is deciding whether "to be or not to be," he is a liminal figure. What is compelling about his thought processes in this moment is that he cannot go back, and the way in which he goes forward will define him. This is true for each of us; in a moment, after we contemplate a deed and choose whether to do it, we will either live as the person who did, or did not, but either way we will be different than we are now.

The same is true for educators and learners in each moment they decide whether to do things differently, with integrity, or just dust off the textbook and answer the questions at the end of the chapter.

In recent decades, it has been exciting to see the flipped classroom, digitally enhanced project-based learning, connected learning, and other "micro-movements" that have effectively broadened the conversation about education by taking risks and doing things in ways that are not associated with the pre-internet closed system classroom.

However, as a profession and as a society, teachers are still in a liminal space, because these practices only address systems of instructional delivery and evaluation. The public does not yet have a framework that clearly articulates the underlying principles of teaching and formal education, so each teacher who develops original learning experiences does so independently.

Educators who innovate in order to create a meaningful learning experience for students are liminal figures because their methods reveal that many of the stories we once believed about school no longer serve students or our society the way they once did. For example, the narrative of the teacher as undisputed content expert and unquestioned authority. Or the narrative that multiple choice tests, percentages, points, and grades tell us about what a learner knows or how well-equipped the learner is to apply that knowledge in the world.

When education leaders stubbornly cling to obsolete narratives, they appear more delusional and less credible to those who need their leadership most. This is true even when educators overextend themselves trying to be kind and supportive.

As Diana, an Open-Source Learning student said: "Failure *is* an option."

Her comment may come as a surprise. Most teachers want students to succeed; their own professional identity is wrapped up in student performance, and they have a bias against failure.

Diana explained what she meant. "Last year I had some hard things happen. My counselor knew I was sad and depressed a lot of the time. My teachers were so nice and caring," she said. "They forgave work I missed and constantly communicated with me and made sure that there was no way I could fail."

She paused. "I never felt like such a baby. It was like they thought I couldn't do anything for myself. I passed. But I wasn't proud of that—it's not like I had a choice. But in this course, everything is up to me. If I don't do my work, or ask questions, I'm going to blow it. That's awesome, because I know that if I succeed, it's because I did it. It's my choice. My success."

That is what a hero sounds like after she passes the threshold.

This is not to say that adults shouldn't offer support; however, the goal should be self-sufficiency, and many students never get there. They internalize and come to believe the old stories: "I was never a good student," "I'm terrible at math," "I can't draw."

In private, many learners and educators admit their frustrations about the constraints of school. But they know they cannot take school on and win, so they stay in their classrooms and avoid attracting attention at meetings. When they do something creative, or fun, or wildly successful beyond anyone's expectations, they feel like they have gotten away with something.

CASE STUDY: TEACHER AS EXECUTIVE, GARDENER, AND BICYCLE MECHANIC

Jesse Grimm is a high school special education teacher on California's Central Coast who described success as "the feeling that I am looking over my shoulder, about to get in trouble."

Grimm created a "transition skills" program. His students created budgets, coded digital tools to measure the soil temperature in the garden they were building, and ran a shop where they repaired bicycles for the P.E. department. Asked to describe his role at the school, Grimm said, "The administration has no idea what I do here."

It is not uncommon for teachers to feel misunderstood by school administrators, who exert increasing pressure on teachers to do work that does not directly benefit students. According to David Graeber, author of *Bullshit Jobs*, "As with almost all teaching positions in the United States . . . the proportion of hours spent teaching in class or preparing lessons has declined, while the total number of hours dedicated to administrative tasks has increased dramatically."[24]

Some of the best school administrators are truly stars—as in, whatever light and heat that people receive from them now was generated years ago in a constellation that no longer exists.

"In the garden," Grimm said, "They (administrators) told me that they felt like kids were just standing around out there, not really being productive."

Meanwhile, Grimm's students mastered subjects and skills including:

- arithmetic
- money management
- writing
- gardening
- how to safely handle and operate power tools
- meditation and focus
- biology
- project management

One of the reasons that Grimm's students achieved so much was their approach to project management. They developed a system to manage their workflow. They used Google calendar to establish timelines and coordinate shared activities and meetings. They used Quicken to manage their budgets for the garden and the bicycle shop. They experimented with a Gantt chart to benchmark their progress, then switched to a Kanban board.

In describing how special education students demonstrated their ability to solve problems and develop project management skills, Grimm said,

> I view Open-Source Learning as the most natural thing—experiential learning and sharing. I grew up working on bicycles, and just brought tools from home on my daily commute in case my bike broke down. A few times it did, and then I would fix it in front of students. Then they wanted to help. I contacted the P.E. department, and we were given access to the bikes, and we worked on keeping them going. This was a daunting process though, because every repair basically had to be bottlenecked through me. This got us thinking about systems of organization. The use of blogs and the public internet really got me thinking about the walled garden, and how limited we were before, and how being more open was a better way to be. Blogs opened up the connections, even for me, actually believing that what I was doing and how I saw the world had value for other people.

The outcomes were positive by any measure. Students were demonstrating skill mastery in practice and on formal assessments. They were actively participating in successful Individual Education Program (IEP) meetings with administrators and family members, who reported that the students were thriving. Mr. Grimm's students matriculated to wood shop, graduation, and the California Institute for the Blind. Grimm also wrote and won two grants for the school.

"Through receiving an Innovation Grant for teaching," Grimm wrote, "I was able to buy Arduino units so my students could learn about circuits, build data-taking instruments for our garden, and create a mix of digital and analog learning experiences that to me represented all aspects of life."

But even in the garden, the nail that sticks up gets hammered. Grimm had the capacity to support students who coped with challenges including schizophrenia, Accutane poisoning, blindness, delusion—once he interrupted a conversation with a colleague to spend thirty minutes patiently and gently convincing a student that it was not in fact 1973—but over time the organizational culture of the school wore him down. "I miss working in the garden and doing the experimental things I did back then," Grimm wrote. "It started to take on a much bigger footprint. . . . As it got bigger. . . . It was as if people were giving me space to create it, only to take it over and make it part of the system."

School appears to be built of stone and certainty, but at its core, school is a system of beliefs. The traditional culture and structure of school is based on assumptions about human nature that lead to conclusions about trust and reliance on hierarchical power to maintain the appearance of positive outcomes.

Grimm said, "Open-Source Learning gave me the feeling that I was doing something right; I could relate my intentions to other types of learning that had already been documented. The conversation was liberating." Connection and collaboration is so important for teachers and learners; more on this in chapter 5 ("The Power of the Network").

In the meantime, the structural and cultural constraints of school present challenges to be navigated. This is where heroes are made.

The teacher, parent, or employer who preserves the messy, productive, and delightful elements of learning becomes a trusted guide and a champion. The learner who dares to ask a Big Question, explores the interdisciplinarity, and curates the journey completes a true rite of passage.

The next two chapters discuss beliefs about effective learning and ways to bring it to the classroom.

Chapter 3

And Yet, It Moves

There are a number of very important irreversibles to be discovered in our universe. One of them is that every time you make an experiment you learn more: quite literally, you can't learn less.

Buckminster Fuller[1]

This is not a classroom, but more of a space, a space that holds endless possibilities.

Vincent Cruz[2]

The apple may not have hit Newton in the head.[3]

Archimedes may not have run naked through the streets of Syracuse shouting, "Eureka!"[4]

Does it matter?

As we explored in the previous chapter, what matters is what we believe.

Many of our beliefs about learning are more positive and productive than our beliefs about school. In fact, some of our favorite beliefs about learning are based on stories that have nothing to do with school.

We have believed and repeated the stories about the "discovery" of gravity by Newton and the theories of volume by Archimedes throughout the generations because they are relatable. How wonderful it is to be able to relate to a historical genius like Newton. According to the legend, Newton gained great insight into the nature of the physical world around us because of a random event—*doink!*—that could have happened to anyone. How satisfying and fun to get an idea in the shower and feel a kinship with Archimedes, one of the greatest mathematicians and scientists of the ancient world, making a discovery and going bananas about it in his bathtub.

Open-Source Learning encourages us to remember that real learning often brings with it a sudden, intense experience of *joy*.

We love discovery. Whether or not the California gold prospectors knew the origin of the word *Eureka* (it's from the ancient Greek for, "I have found it"), their triumphant cries of discovery of gold in 1849 resonated with so many people that the State of California adopted "Eureka" as its official motto. The spirit of the motto lives: witness the school board meeting where everyone set aside their differences long enough to get excited and shout it out loud. For all our differences, the excitement of discovery may be the one remaining thing that everyone in this country has in common.

While discoveries can cure diseases, solve problems, and create opportunities for millions, some of the most personally satisfying discoveries are more immediate. They occur all the time over the course of a day. You answer a trivia question correctly. You make pizza dough for the first time—and it is delicious! You find cash in yesterday's pants pocket before you start the washing machine.

Eureka! Can you *feel* it?

Maybe discovery feels so good because we human beings are so insatiably curious. Researchers who study the human brain have called us informavores[5]—we seek out information and try to make sense of it in the same way that carnivores seek out meat and try to consume it.

In the previous chapter, Festinger's theory of cognitive dissonance illustrated how we try to resolve the discomfort that occurs when things don't seem to make sense. But just as importantly—maybe even more importantly, when it comes to learning new things—we are also highly motivated by the desire to feel good. Thinkers from Epicurus to Freud have cited this "pleasure principle" as a driving force in human behavior.[6]

The drive to resolve contradictions and experience relief, and the drive to explore and experience the joy of discovery are both useful. The more we learn about our learning—not just theories of learning but our own lived experience of learning—the more we can compare the results of our experiments with the stories we have internalized.

PROCESS: THE JOY OF MATH

What do you believe about your own learning? Is it based on factual evidence that you can verify or replicate in the world, or is it a story you have told yourself for a long time and come to accept as true?

Open-Source Learning invites us to question what we think we know about ourselves by experimenting with our talents so that we can better understand where we have aptitude, and where we need to practice and improve. This is especially important in those areas where we think we are weak. As Vincent Van Gogh wrote to his brother Theo, "If you hear a voice within you saying, 'You are not a painter,' then by all means paint, boy, and that voice will be silenced."[7]

Internalizing others' judgements as our own deficiencies is so baked into our cognitive and affective development that we don't even notice it. Many students say they are "bad" at something: writing essays, drawing, understanding science—it can be anything. Math is a major culprit. Many students and adults believe that they are bad at math.

One Open-Source Learning teacher—an English teacher and an accomplished writer who had published curriculum guides, books, and screenplays—told a roomful of teachers at a workshop that she was bad at math. She described how she had gone out of her way to avoid courses that were heavy on math and equations because, in her words, "I told myself that my brain was not 'wired' to think that way."

Here is her story:

"Imagine my surprise as an adult when I found a box of old school papers at my parents' house. My test scores were in there. Up through the sixth grade, my math scores were actually higher than my language scores. This was news to me, and it completely contradicted what I thought I knew about my aptitude for math.

"Where did I get that idea? Why did I think I was bad at math?

"As I mulled this over, I went over every math class I could remember, every teacher, and—oh. Suddenly I understood.

"The belief did not start out as an idea that I was bad at math. It started out that I hated math class. My seventh-grade algebra teacher accused me of cheating on a test in class because I didn't show my work. She made me go to her classroom at lunch and take an extra test that she wrote just to expose my alleged cheating.

"It was just me, her, and her overhead projector. I had to leave all of my belongings at the back of the room and use the pen and paper she gave me. I sat there and answered all of the algebra questions that she wrote on the overhead projector two feet away from me. She sat over me on her stool and watched my every move.

"On principle, I did the calculations in my head. I did not write out any of the steps on the paper.

"She corrected my paper and told me that I got all of the answers right. She also said that she could not understand how I could possibly get the right answers without showing my work.

"She said I had to be cheating. She tore up my paper.

"After that, math class was just something I endured to graduate. I resented the whole shit show, with the sort of energy that only a fourteen-year-old can muster, and I hid my resentment by putting in just enough effort to be invisible.

"As a result, I was not open to coursework or new ideas. I did not learn mathematics well."

According to Stanford Graduate School of Education professor Jo Boaler, "Students learn math best when they approach the subject as something they enjoy."[8]

The teacher eventually internalized the issue as her own: "Over time, somewhere along the way, I began to see my aversion to math as a quality of my own thinking or my aptitude."

Everyone is susceptible to developing beliefs about our own abilities based on our experiences in school. We internalize experience and the opinions of others, especially authority figures, and over time we reinforce these ideas until they become "true." We behave and live accordingly, and then we act as if that in itself proves the case. Most people who think they are bad at art haven't taken an art class or even tried to draw anything in years.

For many learners, the problem with doing well in school is not cognition, language acquisition, or even willingness to learn. It is the fact that schools require individuals to conform to institutional rules of learning, and students succeed or fail based on their ability to adapt and play someone else's game, which often is not aligned with their ability to learn.

As a result, everyone who wants to focus on real learning is made to feel uncomfortable in school. The negative impact on performance is exacerbated when students and teachers have other stressors to contend with, such as poverty, trauma, depression, or anxiety.

On a given day at school, how many people do their best work, as opposed to their "best work under the circumstances"? Under the veneer of school colors and special events, there is often a haze of negativity under the surface on campus. In *Savage Inequalities*, educator and author Jonathan Kozol cited substandard conditions, learning materials, low pay, and biting criticism from the community as factors that contribute to "a mood of cumulative futility."[9]

Countless studies and books have documented how the difficult working conditions and disconnected compensation of being at school creates predictable outcomes. Consider this description of a very successful teacher who left the profession, from *Teachers Have It Easy*: "Were it not for the pay, the time away from his family, and the pervasive sense of being less effective than he wanted to be, he says, he would have been happy teaching for the rest of his career. As it is, he left teaching with no immediate plans to return—and is so disenchanted with public education that he and his wife decided to home-school their own children."[10]

If a teacher or a learner is still in the room, they haven't quit or dropped out, which is a good sign.

If a teacher or a learner is uncomfortable or frustrated, they haven't burned out or given up, which is a really good sign. This person still has energy for the fight and believes that things can and should be better.

Open-Source Learning fuels this fire by giving it oxygen; instead of tamping down differences or disagreements, Open-Source Learning encourages teachers and students to express themselves, air grievances, imagine alternatives, and contribute solutions.

Here are some ways the Open-Source Learning belief system has helped learners transcend traditional barriers to understand and align their natural learning tendencies with their practices and goals.

ALTERING SPACE AND TIME

Disrupting traditional beliefs to make room for new ideas about curiosity and original thinking begins with the physical context of the space and time in which we learn.

Every teacher is an architect. The practice of Open-Source Learning invites students to become co-architects, and to exercise power to influence their physical environment—which, in most schools, is dingy, uninspiring, and begging for an aesthetic ass-kicking.

The design of learning environments must focus on people and how they interact. Former Harvard professor and architecture critic Sarah Williams Goldhagen put it this way: "Design is a social instrument. Built environments shape social relations. This is true for every place that we live and everywhere that we go. So people's experience of the built environment is at once private and individual—situated in our bodies and the natural world—and public, situated in our social worlds."[11]

The built environment in many schools is totally depressing. There is so much to be done with color, texture, sound design, and manipulation of space. Even in a dilapidated portable classroom, it is possible to create moments in space, vignettes that draw people into moments of contemplation, conversation, cooking, or making.

As things stand now for most students, however, the constraints of space and time in school often make learning more difficult. Time is equally important in the design of learning environments. Just as students are settling into their fluorescent-lit boxes and getting warmed up for a discussion, or mustering the courage to raise their hand and ask a clarifying question—suddenly the bell rings and everyone is zipping up backpacks.

Open-Source Learning can constructively disrupt space and time to learners' advantage, without angering the institutional gods and getting punished for the effort, by encouraging learners to reflect on their own learning and collaborate to transform the classroom.

CASE STUDY: DESIGNING FOR LEARNING

One Open-Source Learning course begins the year by greeting students with several blog posts. When the teacher moved to a new classroom, and discovered it in disrepair, he adopted a constructively critical tone and invited them to reimagine their learning environment in a "welcome" post on their course blog.

Students are used to teachers being inauthentically sing-song positive in the face of working conditions that range from inconvenient to awful. The tone of this blog post took students by surprise, because they didn't expect their teacher to be critical—especially not on the first day—and they *definitely* didn't expect their teacher's first words to be, "this classroom sucks."

THIS CLASSROOM SUCKS

When I arrived at the classroom where I'll be teaching this year I was excited. New students, new campus, great to roll my sleeves back up and get my learning on.

Not even the crappy art project painting on the wall outside the door threw me.

But you know, I like choice. I like making a place my own. Even if it's a musty trailer on someone else's lawn. And I walked into this (picture of boxes, stacks of old textbooks, papers, and unplugged computers).

None of this garbage is mine. I don't want it. Now I have to fill out forms and talk to nine different people just to throw it away.

So our first job is to hack our learning environment. I'd like to know in what kinds of places you learn best, and I'd like to know what you'd like to see in here. Sure, I could bring in my posters or make this look like my old classroom, where we had a graffiti wall[12] and about 300 mounted CD cases, but my idea of cool or creative may not look like yours.

We will start this conversation in class tomorrow, and then—unless you want to use that stack of crappy old textbooks—we will post our ideas online and start designing for learning.

* * *

The message disrupted the way students saw their teacher and the classroom. Students are used to seeing a teacher act like something is better than it is, or get upset or angry about bad conditions. This teacher acknowledged reality for what it was, conveyed a sense of aesthetic, and responded to something that did not meet his standards, with a little humor and an edge that added to the excitement of wanting to make things better.

Part of being collegial—that is, part of developing the goodwill that can sustain connections through stress or disagreement—is creating together, and having fun together. The design process provides opportunities to meet both of those needs.

Open-Source Learning design stimulates the imagination. Students have envisioned entire campuses with private, quiet spaces for individual study, open shared spaces for collaboration, industrial workshop spaces for constructing projects, and even a commercial kitchen.

Ideally, the architecture and engineering of any campus should include stakeholder input and design to meet their needs: an urban campus may move into unused retail or manufacturing spaces. A rural campus may be a working farm.

"Great goals," teachers have said in Open-Source Learning workshops, "But I teach in a trailer that is called a 'portable' even though it hasn't moved in nine years." This is understandably frustrating. However, even in the drabbest buildings, it is possible to design elements of the environment in ways that support optimal learning.

One of the most important things we can do in the Open-Source Learning environment is help learners forget that they are sitting captive in a fluorescent-lit box on a fenced-in campus.

Casinos are the undisputed masters of creating physical environments that encourage specific focus and behavior, so take a page out of their playbook.

For starters, remove reminders of the outside world. This helps students remember where they are, by forgetting where they are not.

Here are some ways to accomplish this.

- **Invite the students to redesign the space and make it their room.** This step is one of the most important steps an educator can encourage. Sometimes, the students have great ideas and go nuts decorating. Sometimes they do not. Either way, the room tells a story of the people who spend time there. Surfers spray painted a wall. Techies brought in boxes of electronic junk and tools to create a makerspace. Music lovers brought in hundreds of CD jewel cases. Here, the value of the design is in the experience and the interaction, the interpretation of the space.

  For instance, to one person, a broken vase is a dysfunctional remnant of something that no longer exists. However, in Japan, to a *kintsugi* ("golden joinery") artist, gluing the vase together with lacquer and bright dust that highlights the cracks not only makes it a beautiful object of a different sort, but includes the broken moment in what becomes a visual history of the vase that invites thinking and storytelling. A classroom wall can tell a story just as compellingly, whether it has anything on it or not.

- **Control the temperature.** "How can we do our best when we are physically uncomfortable?" asked a teacher in the San Fernando Valley, near Los Angeles, where the temperature can rise well above 100 degrees in the summer.

  Open-Source Learning teacher Dave Mitchell and his students were baking: "The thermostat was locked, and the maintenance staff did not respond. I remembered my roots and fixed it myself.

  "My first classroom was a portable and the 'repair' was easy. First I picked the lock on the plastic thermostat cover with a paperclip. When I got to class the next day and found the cover had been locked again, I just smashed it.

  "Later, when I taught in a room in one of the main buildings and the thermostat was protected by a digital lock, I researched the model's schematics and the manufacturer online. I called the company and a sympathetic customer service representative walked me through the processes of defeating the lock and resetting the temperature. The next morning word got around that my room was the cool place (literally) to be. My classes won the school award for best attendance that semester."

- **Rearrange the furniture, purposefully, or just because.** Today's class may need to work independently, or focus on the same content at the same time, or participate in a Socratic seminar, or collaborate and talk in smaller groups. Maybe it will all be different tomorrow.

Disrupting routines (such as taking a different way home or brushing your teeth with the other hand) can enhance neurological function in much the same way as learning something new. The brain likes efficiency, and it will revert to what works automatically unless it is challenged. Unless there is a specific accommodation or supportive purpose, there is never a need to assign seats. With rare exceptions, students sit in the same seats every day as a matter of routine. Until the teacher piles all the chairs and desks up on the side of the room. Or someone suggests everyone go outside and learn under the wide open sky.

- **Avoid using materials and constructs that students see in every other classroom.** Bulletin boards only reinforce the conventional. College posters only serve as painful reminders of where students are currently not, yet. Motivational posters are worse. It's just cruel to yell at students during class in big red letters: "You can do anything!!!" when they know full well that they are not even allowed to pee without permission.
- **For crying out loud, let students be in charge of their own bathroom needs.** If your school requires the use of hall passes, put them where students can get them without having to ask for permission. Trust is a key element of Open-Source Learning. No classroom lesson will ever be more compelling than the urgent need to go to the bathroom. Policy should be (a) collaboratively created and (b) made on the assumption that people will do the right thing.

Each of these design principles, and anything else teachers do, should be explicitly acknowledged in discussions with learners so that students can participate in the decision-making process and share their perspectives and ideas.

Each group of learners is unique. The one thing they all have in common is this:

We are here now, and this time and space is like no other that ever was, or will ever be.

That's a classroom worth paying admission to enter.

In that spirit, Open-Source Learning promotes the idea that the learning space is a place we get to be, instead of a place we have to be.

It is exciting when students take the lead in describing problems and brainstorming solutions. Ask them: *What are we doing here? Does this space support that? How can we make it better?*

At the end of a year in an Open-Source Learning classroom, Vince Cruz wrote in his blog about the effect:

"Room 608." Walking up to this "classroom" every day I look right at this number as I approach the door. Although my thought isn't "here we go again" with a drag in my voice it's more of "What lies within?" As said by Forrest Gump, "Life is like a box of chocolates, you never know what you're going to get." Well 608 is the same way. You walk into a seemingly normal classroom and you are instantly struck with a journey. You have a proposed question that instantly brings you to thought.

"So many times for me I don't feel like I'm in Room 608 at Righetti High School, but more so in this room, 608, floating throughout the sky, pinballing around in a never ending space. Just like the mental journey you go on. You have endless amounts of thought and you are literally just pin balling through what your mind comes up with. This is not a classroom, but more of a space, a space that holds endless possibilities.

"You could end up walking out of this space with a great idea that will define your life. Or you could walk out with an essay that you will either be very excited to write, or not so excited, but where you land once you walk out of the space is up to you. This space literally can be seen as the train of thought. . . . Train 608 now boarding, no ticket needed."[13]

For some students, the Open-Source Learning classroom is the one sanctuary where they can think. A senior named Cameron said, "It's like school is this car that drove off the end of a pier, and it's filling with water, and our classroom is the one air pocket inside where I can breathe."

* * *

When teachers take attendance, they are only counting bodies from the neck down. We have no real idea whether students are attending consciously—that is, whether they are directing their concentration or mental energy toward a particular message or resource in the moment.

Paying attention is voluntary. People choose to pay attention; they cannot be coerced. Open-Source Learning recognizes that all real learning is a choice. Students learn to differentiate between *hearing,* as a physiological response, and *listening,* as a conscious process that can be refined and enhanced through practice.

When students improve their listening skills, they process information more effectively, which improves their attitude about the learning experience. When they feel a sense of success, they begin to advocate for conditions that help them concentrate.

Isabel made the comment in class: "When you buy a ticket for a concert, you want the experience, so you pay for a ticket and rearrange your life so you can be there."

Performance venues from the Hollywood Bowl in Los Angeles to the Royal Opera House in London honor the shared effort and commitment between performers and audience members, which is why they enforce rules of etiquette that support everyone's attendance.

If an audience member is late for the opening of the show, they are not allowed in. They must wait for an appropriate moment, like the end of the first scene or musical piece, so that their entrance does not distract anyone else from what they all came to see in the first place.

Students in one Open-Source Learning class debated this practice. Roberto said, "That's not fair. They paid for their ticket, maybe they got stuck in traffic or had an emergency. Why shouldn't they get to go in?"

Theresa answered, "They do get to go in. But it's not like the starting time was a secret, or that they just found out about the performance that morning. They knew the policy when they bought their ticket. Besides, what about all the other people who don't want to deal with them stepping over and blocking their view? They also paid, and they were on time. Add up all the money all those people paid and it's worth a lot more."

Students began to imagine what it would take to make the classroom a performance space for thinking people. Everyone agreed that since class began with journal writing, which required concentration, those who arrived up on time should expect some protection from interruptions. Some asked questions: Would a "no late admission" policy make a difference? Would it allow them to focus on their ideas and thought processes? Would it help them perform at a higher level?

Students enthusiastically discussed and debated the topic. At this point, whatever they decided, it would be their decision. The few students who defended their desire to be late were practically laughed out of the room; they quickly admitted they were testing the water. The group as a whole decided that five minutes was a reasonable amount of time to sink in, focus, and start writing. They also agreed that life happens, and sometimes being late cannot be avoided, so there would be no hard feelings about it, but the door would close at the late bell and stay closed for five minutes. This would allow students who arrived on time to consider the journal prompt, settle in, and start writing. At five minutes after the bell, the door would open and late arrivals could quietly take their seats.

The next day, late students found a posted sign on the closed door: "Writers at work. If you are late or visiting, please don't knock on the door or open it for the first five minutes of the period."

The student-led policy created a quiet moment at the beginning of each period, which opened up a new opportunity. Someone asked about yoga and meditation, which led to online research about how meditation influences concentration and focus. Students requested "a minute of mindfulness" in which they could create an atmosphere of quiet and sink into a meditative space.

This was only possible because for a few blissful minutes, no one was knocking on the door or letting it slam as they stumbled into the room and dropped their backpacks.

The students in these classes who adopted the meditation practice immediately improved the quality of their journal writing and their scores on reading-comprehension assessments. Their results are consistent with findings published by researchers at the University of California Santa Barbara, who found that "Mindfulness training improved both GRE reading-comprehension scores and working memory capacity while simultaneously reducing the occurrence of distracting thoughts during completion of the GRE and the measure of working memory."[14]

In this example, creating space for collaborative conversations about process led to identifying needs, which led to discussion and advocacy, which led to new routines, which led to thinking differently about the way learners experience the Open-Source Learning space they occupy together. The physical characteristics of the space are secondary to the intention with which the space is considered and used.

* * *

Making conscious choices about where to direct our attention helps us use time more effectively. One Open-Source Learning class wanted to focus on the present and went so far as to tape up a sign that covered the classroom clock; the sign read. "It's Time."

When students think about time in school, they usually associate it with being late, missing deadlines, or failing to complete a task. They rarely explore how to put the 86,400 seconds in a 24-hour day to the best use.

But what if unforeseen circumstances destroy the time boundaries and schedules at school? How will we determine what to do with our time? Sometimes the most exciting discoveries are those that challenge concepts we previously regarded as fixed or permanent.

For instance, in school, learning is artificially divided by time: during one hour, students must think about mathematics. During the next hour, they must forget about mathematics and think about literature. Then, when the next bell rings, stop thinking about literature because now they must focus only on chemistry. If a question or an idea occurs during chemistry about math or literature later—too bad: it is too late, wait until tomorrow.

In case anyone forgets what they are supposed to be thinking about in the moment, a bell rings—or a loud beep, on one school campus that looked and sounded like a prison.

Ringing bells has been proven effective in training dogs, but the practice does not support developing thoughtful people. When Pavlov research documented how the stimulus of bells became associated with dogs' responses, the effect he demonstrated was not psychological. It was physiological. Writing in *The New Yorker*, Michael Specter observed, "Pavlov's research originally had little to do with psychology . . . that research won him the 1904 Nobel Prize in Physiology or Medicine."[15]

Subsequent research has shown that it is the body's somatic response to routine that drives the behavioral response to this kind of stimulus—not personality, cognition, or emotion.

When students in a classroom hear the bell ring to signal the end of the period, and they begin rustling their bags and getting ready to leave whether they have been dismissed or not, their response to the bell is not located in their conscious thought process, but somewhere else in their physical nervous system. This is an example of schooling rituals that train people to act without thinking.

Learning does not operate on a bell schedule. We get ideas throughout the day and night. We constantly learn, even if we are anticipating something in the future or reflecting on an event in our past.

One of the chief advantages of Open-Source Learning is the freedom it gives learners to process and articulate their thinking at any hour of the day.

THE INTERDISCIPLINARITY

As Ray Kurzweil wrote in *The Singularity is Near*, "As with all of our other institutions we will ultimately move toward a decentralized education system in which every person will have ready access to the highest quality knowledge and instruction.

"The nature of education," said Kurzweil, "will change once again when we merge with nonbiological intelligence. We will then have the ability to download knowledge and skills, at least into the nonbiological portion of our intelligence. Our machines do this routinely today."[16]

The Singularity—in Kurzweil's words, "a future period during which the pace of technological change will be so rapid, its impact so deep, that human life will be irreversibly transformed"[17]—may not be far off, but most of us do not see the development of artificial intelligence as something that is within our control.

However, we can control how we think, and in this moment we can decide to look at any given question through a variety of disciplines and perspectives. This is what Open-Source Learning defines as the Interdisciplinarity—the way in which our understanding is enriched by examining an idea or a skill *through multiple lenses*. The practice has enriched humanity for centuries.

In fourteenth-century Italy, for example, the Medici family expanded its wealth and influence by connecting diverse interests and people. The results produced political power, economic wealth, and innovation that contributed to the Renaissance.

Author Frans Johansson coined the term "the Medici Effect" to describe what happens when people of different backgrounds examine a question or a problem through a fresh perspective. Teachers may not serve as patrons for the likes of Galileo, Michelangelo, or da Vinci, but teachers can certainly facilitate the kinds of interaction that break down what Johansson calls "associative boundaries":

"If we just ask different questions about a problem, we can see it in a new light," said Johansson. "Leonardo da Vinci, the defining Renaissance man and perhaps the greatest intersectionalist of all times, believed that in order to fully understand something one needed to view it from at least three different perspectives."[18]

We see the impact of the Medici Effect on innovation throughout our culture. Among many recent high-profile examples of interdisciplinary thinkers, consider Steve Jobs, who famously studied art and calligraphy, and went on to design some of the world's most influential devices even though he had little technological expertise.

In David Edwards' book *Artscience*, he describes the effect that occurs when thinkers apply thinking from one field to another:

"These translators may see the beat of healthy hearts as reflective of the note patterns in classical music, like cardiac specialist Ary Goldberger, whose work also includes information analysis of the plays of Shakespeare; or they may see mathematics in art, like Benoit Mandelbrot, whose invention of fractal geometry has helped artists and scientists probe more deeply into the beauty and complexity we encounter in nature."[19]

Thinking interdisciplinarily and innovatively is how we will eventually cure cancer, and create broad national and international agendas that bring together thousands of people in extraordinarily diverse fields for unified missions—like preserving the climate of Earth for future generations of human inhabitants.

However, it is not easy to integrate these paths in a world of specialization because of the psychological habits we develop, and the institutional barriers that arise between organizations and schools of thought.

It's even tougher within the structured study in the traditional classroom. School is the only place where we divide life into artificially defined subjects.

Life is interdisciplinary. A cup of tea is a study in botany, ceramics, Chinese mythology, fluid mechanics, and the history of colonialism. A wedding picture is a master class in biology, probability, economics, poetry, music, culinary arts, psychology, and much more.

Every question we ask is interdisciplinary and can be viewed in terms of multiple academic subjects.

In the classroom, an all-encompassing statement such as "every question we ask" is an invitation to smartassery. Because Open-Source Learning invites students to consider themselves colleagues of the teacher, it is not unusual for a student to respond to this invitation by saying something like, "Oh, yeah? OK, here is my Big Question: May I go to the bathroom?"

The Open-Source Learning approach here is to take the question at face value and engage: "Sure. Every question really is interdisciplinary. So, if asking permission to use the bathroom is really your Big Question, let's start by considering ways to think about it."

Make a list:

- Psychology of power and autonomy
- Biology
- Plumbing
- Anthropology
- Sustainability and water conservation, and of course,
- The grammar of "can" versus "may"

Engaging in this way is a useful step in the Open-Source Learning process. Students need to push the boundaries and still be taken seriously. The conversation itself is a learning experience.

It does not matter whether the teacher is personally interested in the topic. It matters that the teacher is interested in the student's interest in the topic. A teacher who gets a sarcastic answer can respond in exactly the same way they would to a serious inquiry.

Students quickly realize that the teacher's offer to help them investigate anything they choose is sincere. Often this brings them back to the drawing board in order to think about what really matters to them.

In the end, Open-Source Learning validates what students have long suspected: learning is not limited by space, time, or traditional academic subjects.

Open-Source Learning legitimizes learners' experiences—if they still feel like insurgents at school, at least they are now part of a movement. By honestly investigating reality as they experience it, they stand on the shoulders of giants and join a tradition of fearless inquiry. Socrates was given the death penalty for refusing to give up teaching. Reportedly, his last words were, "The unexamined life is not worth living." After Galileo was persecuted for more than twenty years at the hands of the Roman Inquisition, Galileo was found guilty and ordered, on pain of torture, to recant the heliocentric Copernican theory that the Earth revolves around the Sun.

Ultimately, Galileo caved to the demands of the church, but not in his heart. According to Ivar Ekeland, the chair of mathematical economics of the University of British Columbia, "This is the true Galilean revolution. It is told that, after kneeling down in front of the tribunal to foreswear the Copernican view that the Earth moves around the Sun, Galileo touched the ground while standing up and said, 'And yet, it moves!'"[20]

* * *

Mindful encouragement of interdisciplinarity is at the heart of developing a culture of Open-Source Learning in the classroom.

Here is a blog post frequently used in Open-Source Learning to introduce the Big Question as a core component of the experience.

Following the posts are some of the students' actual Big Questions. Every Big Question is a good start. It is a valuable first step in reinforcing—you could say rehabilitating—students' ability to ask questions that will guide their explorations in ways that they can't in the traditional classroom.

(For a link to an online version of this post, which includes images, videos, all of the students' comments, and links to the sources that are cited in this post, see page 150.)

WHAT'S YOUR BIG QUESTION?

Our minds are naturally inclined toward associative and interdisciplinary thinking. We connect the dots in all sorts of ways, often when we don't fully comprehend the experience (and sometimes when there aren't even any dots).

We have questions about the nature of the world: our experience of it, our place in it, our relationship to it, what lies beyond it, and everything else. When we're young, we ask questions all the time. We are insatiably curious. It's like somehow we intuitively understand that the more we learn the better we get at everything—including learning. We don't worry about curricular units or standards. We have no test anxiety. We test ourselves all the time. We love risk and we don't care if we fail.

It's always somebody else who's saying, "Hey, come down from there, you're going to get hurt!"

Not only do we love climbing learning limbs when we're young, we know it's what we're best at.

We have every incentive to accelerate and amplify our learning as we age. Our future is increasingly complex and uncertain. Our culture and economy favor those in the know. Learning is increasingly your responsibility as individuals. You're becoming more independent; soon you'll be heading off to college, where your professors may not know you exist and definitely won't care how you organize your binder.

As if all that isn't motivation enough for you to get your learning on, it turns out that not learning may actually be bad for you. We form new neurons and connections in our brains when we learn. Scientists are investigating whether the lack of new neuron formation is a cause for depression or an interfering factor in recovery.

When it comes to thinking for yourself in the traditional high school setting, though, there are constraints. The fear of punishment or embarrassment can lead the smartest and most successful learners to surrender and play the game. When this happens, motivated learning in the presence of no opportunity dies the same death as a fire in the presence of no oxygen. The authors of "The Creativity Crisis"[21] say we ask about 100 questions a day as preschoolers—and we quit asking questions altogether by middle school.

Richard Saul Werman, the man who created the TED conference, said, "In school we're rewarded for having the answer, not for asking a good question." School and the way it works was designed back when things were very different and oriented around mass production; that's not the way the world works any more.

You can't just prepare for a job that may not be around by the time you graduate. In the age of the search engine, there is no real point in learning facts for their own sake, especially since so many of them eventually turn out not to be facts after all.

You have to develop the critical thinking, problem-solving, opportunity-seeking, and collaborative skills that will enable you to CREATE a role for yourself in the new economy. (And don't worry, if you're not an entrepreneur by nature, these abilities will help you do whatever else you want to do more effectively.)

Our first mission is to reclaim the power of the question. Everything you ask has an interdisciplinary answer. No matter what the question or the answers, you're going to have to sort the signal from the noise and determine how best to share the sense you make.

What have you always wanted to know? What are you thinking about now that you've been asked? What answers would make a difference in your life, or in the community, or in the world? What do you wish you could invent? What problem do you want to solve?

This is not a trick and there are no limits. Please comment to this post with your question and post it to your course blog (title: MY BIG QUESTION). You can always change your question or ask another.

SAMPLE STUDENT COMMENTS

Brenna M.—What is the reason for knowledge being the primary determining factor of our intelligence level, but not imagination or creativity? (Inspired by Albert Einstein)

Carly—What happens beyond space? It has to end somewhere, right?

Lisa K.—Does everyone see colors the same way? As in, we all see grass as "green," but perhaps everyone perceives "green" differently?

Miki K.—How am I going to die? (Plane crash, disease, old age?) How long is forever?

Hannah S.—Why are we as humans so dependent on love? Is it possible to live a fulfilling, rewarding life without loving or being loved in return?

Maddie K.—How do we determine what is right and what is wrong? Decisions we make at different points in time may seem right in that moment, but is it really the best choice? With college applications coming up, this has been on my mind lately.

Allyson B.—If mirrors or clear reflections didn't exist, would there still be a concept of beauty and ugliness? Would people risk comparing the appearances of others when they are unfamiliar with their own?

Carlos—If our ancestors had decided that rocks and dirt were valuable instead of diamonds and oil, would we be fighting wars over gravel right now?

Helio—If we all lived in a " perfect" world would there be such a thing as true happiness, or would it just be considered the normal day-to-day feeling? Would life be boring if nothing went wrong, and there was no excitement? Does having rough patches in life truly help us become better and wiser individuals?

MEDIA AND INFORMATIONAL RESOURCES

Part of the appeal of Galileo's story is that he did not compromise his intellectual integrity. Galileo knew that he was being told to go along with a belief system that did not align with his carefully documented observations of reality.

Today, school communities are told to go along with the belief that school leaders have a clue about how to use and manage technology.

They don't.

Today learners have many choices when it comes to selecting information (for more resources on this, see page 149). But just one generation ago, things were very different, and the result is that today's educators view the world through a different lens than today's learners. Understanding media—how it flourishes and changes, and especially how it has become an increasingly two-way phenomenon—is a key to building the Open-Source Learning experience.

One of the most striking things about digital culture is the way we use familiar metaphors to describe unfamiliar concepts. A section of a computer display that shows the program currently being used is not the same thing as an opening in a wall that admits light, but we call them both windows. At first this may seem lazy, but as George Lakoff and Mark Johnson discuss in *Metaphors We Live By*, "Metaphor is not just a matter of language, that is, of mere words. On the contrary, human *thought processes* are largely metaphorical. Metaphors as linguistic expressions are possible precisely because there are metaphors in a person's conceptual system."[22]

Given what we know about neuroplasticity, and the fact that the wiring of our brains can change with the introduction of new information and habituated routines, it stands to reason that this generation's thinking patterns are different, if only because habitually consuming digital information is different than consuming analog information.

The biggest difference between analog and digital media is that analog has a beginning, middle, and end. Are you old enough to remember the sticker on videotapes at rental stores? "Be kind, rewind." In an analog world, you have to go through one song at a time, or one scene to get to the next.

In digital media, you can zap right to a selection without any sense of context. There is no "before" or "after."

This type of media access changes the ways we tell stories, which changes our belief systems and the way we think. As Marshall McLuhan famously put it, "The medium is the message."

For example, until recently "taking pictures" meant using a camera with film that had to be sent away to be developed. Today, of course, anyone with a smart phone can capture an unlimited number of digital images that are available immediately and shared instantly on social media.

The act of telling the stories of our pictures was a way to connect with the people we cared about and strengthen our memories of shared experiences—such as the neighbor who returned from a vacation and would invite everyone on the street for a travel slide show over dessert. Today, pictures continue to be pictures, but with digital cameras and images, our orientation to them and the way we experience and use them is different.

When we post images, whether someone knows us well or just met us, they can see what we do, what we like, where we go, and what we eat. Our pictures create impressions; others who view our lives online come to "know" our identities through our photo streams.

Producing all of that data, especially on social media platforms owned by companies that sell our information to advertisers, has reversed the flow of information. Instead of looking for information that we need, information comes looking for us, whether we need it or not.

The information that we see in our feeds—take a moment to consider *that* metaphor!—appears by design. As Cathy O'Neil wrote in *Weapons of Math Destruction*,

> We are ranked, categorized, and scored in hundreds of models, on the basis of our revealed preferences and patterns. This establishes a powerful basis for legitimate ad campaigns, but it also fuels their predatory cousins: ads that pinpoint people in great need and sell them false or overpriced promises. They find inequality and feast on it. The result is that they perpetuate our existing social stratification, with all of its injustices.[23]

OPEN-SOURCE LEARNING: A WEAPON
TO FIGHT DISINFORMATION

Because we now receive so much information that is tailored to our lifestyles, and we do not receive any training on how to filter this information, we are susceptible to believing things that are not true, and sometimes even dangerous. Learning to evaluate the credibility of online information is an integral element of Open-Source Learning—and a skill with lifelong benefits.

Internet agenda-setters have become more sophisticated in their messaging, and today's learners must level up in order to understand and evaluate what they see online. For example, if you search for the suffix, "-ology," you will almost certainly see the straightforward definition—"ology" means "the study of"—but you will also see sample sentences from sites that appear to be credible. One sentence that appears in searches is a quote: "No 'ism or 'ology has ever established any scientific principle which has contributed to the general welfare of the people."[24]

"That is so bizarre," you think, as you click on the website that contains the sentence.

The link takes you to a credible dictionary site that teachers have used and endorsed for student use. But when you look closely, you realize the quote comes from a book on maintaining racial purity through marriage and eugenics, a racist school of thought that was debunked over a century ago.

One random sentence may not turn a viewer into a racist idiot, but the appearance of the idea and the source title on a credible website normalizes the concept and gives it a seat at the conversational table. Some ideas have no legitimate place in civil discourse, and this digital back door is open to many people who are unaware of its influence.

These changes in our information culture highlight the need to rebalance our thinking and our habits in engaging with information and the media that deliver it to us.

Open-Source Learning addresses this head-on. Students learn about informational constructs that never existed before the public internet. They examine "filter bubbles" that use algorithms to determine what we see in our online feeds based on our search histories, affiliations, likes, purchases, and other digital bread crumbs to make assumptions about what we want to see and deliver content accordingly. Comparing the same news stories as delivered through the filters of different filter bubbles can help us understand how neighbors on the same street can feel like they are living in different worlds.

Students also learn to remix existing messages using different media to create tone and context, and we analyze the effect this has on our understanding of meaning. For example, several years ago during a fight on campus, a law enforcement officer hit a female student and knocked her to the ground. The incident was captured in pictures and video, and the images were seen around the world, online, and in traditional media, including television stations and newspapers from Seoul to London.

In class, students watched the video from a local news station's coverage with the source volume off. The first time, it was accompanied by "Gimme Shelter" by the Rolling Stones; the second time, it was accompanied by "Hallelujah" by Leonard Cohen.

Students raised their eyebrows and said they felt like they had just seen two different stories. The first version of the story seemed raw and angry; the second felt more serene and wistful. This feedback is especially powerful in light of the fact that, just the day before, some of these same students *had witnessed the event in person* from just a few feet away.

For decades, this era has been called the Information Age. In the Information Age, high school and college graduates who are considered "educated" should be able to find, analyze, evaluate, synthesize, and act on the best information out there. These are precisely the strengths that Open-Source Learning helps build.

Chapter 4

Introducing Open-Source Learning in the Classroom

We now accept the fact that learning is a lifelong process of keeping abreast of change. And the most pressing task is to teach people how to learn.

Peter Drucker

Bringing Open-Source Learning into the classroom is a balancing act. Every teacher already knows the feeling of wishing there was more time in the day to

- Connect with students
- Reflect on performance and share feedback
- Complete thoughts and finish discussions that got interrupted
- Answer everyone's questions

Connecting once a week for one minute with each student in a class of forty requires eight minutes with eight students each day in every class. If we add in a few seconds of transition (and interruption) time per conversation, that adds up to ten to twelve minutes per fifty minute class period, or more than 20 percent of class time, and forty minutes with forty different people every day of the week.

Open-Source Learning requires so much more: consulting with students; reading journals, essays, and blog posts; connecting students with mentors; the list goes on.

Doing all of that—not to mention balancing institutionally required tasks such as testing and meetings—in a traditional, autocratic way would be wildly impractical. Therefore, Open-Source Learning elicits participation and cultivates collaboration from the beginning.

On the first day of school, Open-Source Learning is presented as one of several options.

On the second day of school, students are asked to write about the most memorable experiences from the first day.

Here is one student's journal entry that captures the flavor of the experience:

> *The most memorable moment from Monday was how free the class seemed. There were no lines you had to walk on and no one was holding your hand. We would actually be independent and this helps us test how responsible we can actually be. The teacher gave us options (as a class) on what to decide. Instead of influencing us to do his preference, he decided to step aside for a couple of minutes and let us discuss as a class. In the end we called the teacher back and told him we decided on Open-Source Learning.*
>
> *Jimena*

The first day of a new learning experience is the perfect opportunity to invite people to an adventure. Calling classroom learning "an adventure" may seem like an exaggeration, but Open-Source Learning seems like a bold undertaking to students who are used to being treated like intellectual veal—that is, kept quiet and still in small boxes and allowed to do only what authority figures tell them.

Creating an atmosphere where students can choose their own adventure requires something unexpected.

The most unexpected thing a student can encounter on the first day of school is being vested with the power to say "no" to a teacher's presentation and to self-determine how a course will run. Rather than send a syllabus home for a parent to sign, the Open-Source Learning teacher begins by modeling a belief that appears radical to people who don't associate it with school: trust.

To be clear: trust in this sense goes beyond, "I trust you to not steal my car keys from my desk." The trust described here creates a bond between people that allows them to explore new ideas, to make mistakes, and to disagree without disconnecting.

THE FIRST DAY OF OPEN-SOURCE LEARNING

As Will Rogers famously observed, "You never get a second chance to make a first impression." In most classrooms, the first day is all about rules and expectations.

Clarifying expectations and emphasizing rules provides necessary structure, but in ways that are far from empowering or encouraging. Most school rules set a tone of mistrust and fear: the conventional wisdom says that if a student does not follow directions, they will get in trouble; if a teacher backs off for a second or misses a detail, semi-feral young people and their parents will run wild and get everyone in trouble. These implied messages are disheartening.

Open-Source Learning takes a different approach, by speaking directly to the students' experience and acknowledging everyone's fears out loud.

Kathy Griggs, a teacher in an urban high school on the East Coast, introduced Open-Source Learning this way:

"Hi everyone. We haven't met, but I know one thing about you: you have been in school for more than ten years, and that makes you a veteran in this organization.

"I'm going to make a guess. You have seen The First Day of School Show many times, and you know the routine: you get a syllabus, a textbook, and a lecture about asking permission to talk or use the bathroom.

"Maybe some of you have had different kinds of experiences. Raise your hands if you have ever had an enthusiastic teacher who got your attention and made a class seem like it was going to be different."

Griggs looked around the room. Some hands went up.

"That's great—I'm glad to hear it. Keep your hands up if it stayed that way."

All the hands went down.

"Am I understanding this right? A few times on the first day, you got a message that made you think the class would be different, but then after a few weeks it was just the same old thing?"

By now all the students were nodding, including people who had not raised their hands or responded to anything yet.

"How did that make you feel?"

Some students began to talk: "Bored. Disrespected. Pissed off."

"Alright, I hear you. And I feel a little hopeful and a little challenged. Because the truth is, I have no idea yet how this course is going to be for you. I can tell you one thing. You have more power here than you think."

Griggs watched as some students nodded. Some gave quizzical glances that indicated the course had crossed into unfamiliar territory.

"Some of what I am about to say may sound like an exaggeration, like it is too good to be true—which is why I have the projector set up."

As Griggs described Open-Source Learning, she showed examples of previous course blogs, student-led adventures, and a student video. Then, she stopped and apologized.

"I have already taken up too much of your time by talking. Your time is valuable. Do you know what opportunity cost is? Right now, you are giving up every other possibility to be here—you could be taking a nap, petting your dog, skydiving—and at the end of this hour you're going to be an hour closer to the end of your life. There is no do-over, so I want to make sure you feel like it was time well-spent. And right now you have a decision to make."

Griggs defined "consensus," and explained why it is the strongest type of decision a group can make, and also the most difficult to achieve. Not only did everyone have to agree, they had to mean it. They had to *commit*. They could not settle for the false comfort of giving in to the majority for the sake of making the decision faster or avoiding disagreement. They had to back their agreement with their total support, because from then on they would have to live with it for the entire school year.

She drove the point home by telling students, "There is no back row on the internet where you can slouch down and try to be invisible—in the transparent world of Open-Source Learning, not producing content is as conspicuous as producing great content."

Griggs then promised everyone a free pizza lunch—as long as they could agree on the toppings. Inevitably, a student attempted to sacrifice truth for pizza. This often happens. When the debate intensifies, someone tries to resolve the conflict and support the group by agreeing to a topping that they privately plan to pick off.

Open-Source Learning reveals each participant's level of commitment. There is no back row on the internet where students can hunch down and act like they are invisible.

Considering an entirely new approach to learning and participating in a decision that will impact the rest of the school year is a lot to ask of students, especially on the first day of school.

Griggs understood that achieving real consensus takes time, so she told students that making this decision is the only job they had, no matter how long it took. As of that moment, their entire grade for the semester depended on their ability to execute this task. Nothing else would be proposed until they decided. How could it be otherwise? Until the students chose a course of action, no one could possibly know what would happen next.

Before inviting the students to take over the discussion, Griggs asked if anyone has any questions or needed any additional information that will help them with their decision.

Of course, just having the teacher in the room creates pressure, because when students are aware of being observed by an authority figure they change their conduct. For this reason, Griggs told the students that she was going outside. She asked the class to send someone to tell her when they reached a verdict.

Then she walked out of the room.

Imagine the scene on the other side of the classroom door when it slammed and the students found themselves alone and in charge.

Open-Source Learning teachers never wait more than a few minutes, and the answer is always the same. The students are intrigued by the promise of doing something new, and they are taken aback in a good way by the amount of trust the teacher shows in (a) leaving the decision up to them and (b) leaving them to make the decision on their own.

Griggs walked back in and put the course blog she created in advance up on the screen in front of the room for students to see. Now they were ready to talk about what would happen next.

Griggs invited students to copy or take pictures of the course blog URL and his email address. She asked students to bring a spiral notebook or a composition book to class the next day because they would start each day by listening to music and writing on paper, which exercises a different part of the brain than digital media.

Before the class period ended, Griggs asked students to take a few moments later in the day to visit the course blog and comment to a post entitled, "Will This Blog See Tomorrow?" This was a request, not "homework" or an "assignment."

The effect of asking the students to publish their endorsements online was to position them as invested decision-makers. It also set a precedent; owned their words in public where everyone could read them.

When students read what Griggs wrote, they saw an accurate description of what they had just experienced. Suddenly, the internet resembled reality. The course blog seemed more like the social media they recognized from life outside of school.

Here is a similar post in which a teacher documents the first-day conversation, followed by a few student comments that represent the sentiments of the class (to see an unabridged version of this post online, complete with source links and dozens of student comments, follow the link in the title's endnote). The blog post is intended as a reading experience, an exploratory exercise in using on digital media, and a teachable moment about user terms and agreements. Students don't just click a box to indicate their agreement; by commenting in their own words, they make the document and experience their own.

WILL THIS BLOG SEE TOMORROW?[1]

It's an open question. Think about today's in-class discussion, ask yourself what you really want out of this semester, and then comment to this post with your decision and at least one reason for it. (NOTE: As Benjamin Franklin famously observed, "We all hang together or we all hang separately." We won't move forward unless all of us participate.)

The model of "Open-Source Learning" is defined with a mouthful: "A guided learning process that combines timeless best practices with today's tools in a way that empowers learners to create interdisciplinary paths of inquiry, communities of interest and critique, and a portfolio of knowledge capital that is directly transferable to the marketplace."

Students use Open-Source Learning to create a wild variety of personal goals, Big Questions, Collaborative Working Groups, and online portfolios of work that they can use for personal curiosity, self-improvement, or as a competitive advantage in applying for jobs, scholarships, and admission to colleges and universities. Check out a sample course blog and some personal member blogs. (See page 150.)

The defining characteristic of Open-Source Learning is that there is no chief; all of us are members of a network that is constantly evolving. Another key element is transparency. What we learn and how well we learn it, how we respond to setbacks, and even some of our favorite inspirations and habits of mind are right out there in public for everyone to see. Readers will rightly perceive what we curate as the best we have to offer.

All of this is Open. In thermodynamics, an open system exchanges substance, not just light and heat. To us, the important idea is that the network can change in composition and purpose. Every time you meet someone new and exchange ideas, you're not only enriching each other, you're changing your minds and contributing opportunities for others to do the same. In other words, you're learning and teaching* (*one of the most effective ways to learn).

We're not limited to one source for curriculum or instruction. We have a full slate of online conferences scheduled this year including authors, authorities on the internet and social media, entrepreneurs, and others. One year a mother/daughter team presented a lesson on class distinctions in Dickens and Dr.

Seuss online. Another student invited a champion drummer to talk with students online about music and its connections to literature and life. As you get the hang of this you'll come up with your own ideas. Testing them will give you a better sense of how to use the experience to your greatest advantage.

Improving your own mind is the highest form of success in this course of study.

As you know, many people are worried about the use of technology in education (*Put that phone away or I'll confiscate it!*). They are rightly concerned about safety, propriety, and focus: will learners benefit or will they put themselves at risk? As we move forward, you will learn how the internet works, how you can be an effective online citizen, and how you can use digital tools to achieve your personal and professional goals. You'll also learn a lot about writing and the habits of mind that make readers and writers successful communicators.

Because Open-Source Learning is a team sport, this is all your call. You have to decide if you want to pursue this new direction, or if you prefer the familiarity of the traditional approach. There is admittedly something comforting about the smell of an old book, even if it's a thirty-pound textbook that spent the summer in a pile of lost-and-found P.E. clothes. My perspective may be obvious but I'm just one voice. Please add yours with a comment below.

Sample Student Comments:

Sierra S.—The concept of Open-Source Learning is something new and different that has never before been offered in any of my other classes. Being more interactive through technology and social media will not only help relate to our generation but also put a different spin on how I learn the material. I really like how the course is going to be more dependent on the students. Open-Source Learning will help prepare me for college and the real world where not everything is structured and things are more open to one's own interpretation.

Haley S.—I like the idea of not learning out of a textbook. Open-Source Learning seems like a new and inventive way to redefine the classroom setting and make it more interactive among students. I like that it is student-driven. I am excited to see how much I grow in response to Open-Source Learning.

Joey B.—Every teacher asks what we expect from the upcoming school year or semester and from what I've learned about Open-Source Learning this question is not the same as in other classes. It doesn't ask just for the sake of asking but rather to change to fit our expectations and needs.

Omar D.—This will be the change in my learning that will have me waking up wanting to go to school. It seems that after being in this system since the first grade I have lost the motivation to learn for myself, I learn because I am told to learn in order to be successful. I am tired of a system that forces me to learn things that I will never use in real life or help me develop as a better person. This class will spark something that was extinguished long ago.

Jhaicelle L.—I am very excited about Open-Source Learning because it's very different from what we have been taught all throughout our education. I am also thrilled about getting to use technology in ways I haven't for school because let's face it technology is here and it's not going anywhere. It scares me that I actually might have to think for myself, but I am ready to stand to the challenge.

* * *

The blog post and the comments illustrate how transparency in Open-Source Learning generates engagement, commitment, and data. It is inspiring to see high school students on the first day of school rave about sinking their teeth into learning. This sort of reaction is consistent throughout the Open-Source Learning experience.

In true open-source development style, it is easy to replicate and customize this approach. Speaking directly to the issues, presenting clear information, and making specific requests leads students to think, participate, and write. Teachers can adapt the style of this presentation and process to fit their personalities, the unique needs of their students, and their school's culture.

Declaring intentions contributing comments makes the first impression of Open-Source Learning real and lasting. It also strengthens the likelihood that learners will take next steps. According to Robert Cialdini, author of *Influence*, "One reason that written testaments are effective in bringing about genuine personal change is that they can so easily be made public."[2] Open-Source Learning students take this a step further on Day One by making their own writing public.

Students are more likely to take a risk when they see the teacher go first. Reciprocity is a powerful motivator, but many teachers struggle with taking the leap of faith and putting their trust in students. One teacher at a workshop asked, "What if a student makes a negative comment?"

So? What if they do? Any blog author can moderate or remove comments, but engagement is a golden opportunity to teach the "netiquette" of virtual communities (more on that in the next chapter). Besides, maybe the student has a good point. Maybe the comment will illustrate a misunderstanding, or an opportunity to learn how to improve communication. Maybe the comment will be flat-out wrong or inappropriate. All of these are opportunities to learn, and also chances to make mistakes and model how we can understand and help each other through moments that are less than perfect.

The idea of dignifying errors to promote learning is a recognized best practice in American teaching. According to Madeline Hunter, who is well known in schools of education for inventing the seven-step lesson plan that so many teachers still use today, "Most students will participate more enthusiastically and will venture more responses in your class if they know that not only will you maintain their dignity but in doing so, you'll also help them learn more and remember it longer."[3]

This is one of those points where the conscious application of courage—experiencing the reluctance and taking the risk anyway—is essential.

Besides, many fears about students are completely unfounded.

Open-Source Learning teachers see countless examples of students who do the right thing when they think no one is watching. Every time we put our trust in students, we are richly rewarded. In an Open-Source Learning culture, even when students do the wrong thing, everyone learns from the experience in ways that allow us to maintain connection and continue exploring together.

DESPERATE TO DO THE RIGHT THING

Daniel was a student at James Monroe High School in Los Angeles who earned average grades and better-than-average citizenship marks on his report cards.

Daniel's mother drove him to school, but her car was notoriously unreliable, so he was often late. On the day the school administration decided to "crack down on tardies" and locked the gates at the last morning bell, Daniel was not in class. He missed the next day as well. A rumor circulated that Daniel had an accident, but no one knew details. Daniel was out the rest of the week.

Daniel returned the following Thursday. He was pale and there were dark bags under his eyes. There was a thick bandage on his hand.

The story was more awful than anyone imagined.

Daniel's mother had trouble starting her car on the first day of the new policy, and she arrived at the school just as the security guards were closing the gate. Daniel ran from the car and begged the guards to let him in. The guards refused and told him to walk around the campus to see if the other gate was still open. Daniel knew that by the time he got there, the guards at that entrance would make him go to the gym and sit in detention.

Daniel and a friend, who was also trying to find a way in so he could get to class, decided to climb the school's ten-foot chain link fence, which was topped with rolls of razor wire. His friend went first, made it over, and Daniel followed.

Just as Daniel put his sweatshirt over the concertina wire at the top of the fence, his friend yelled that security was coming. Daniel got distracted. He caught his ring—the school ring he had just bought to celebrate his upcoming graduation—on the wire, which sliced his finger clean off. When security caught up with him, they took him to the nurse and then suspended him for jumping the fence.

Daniel made up every assignment he missed and earned an A in the course. He never found his ring.

SAFETY FIRST

Embracing the concept of "open" is easier for a person who feels safe and secure. No wonder open culture has been mostly promoted by white, educated, upper-middle-class software developers and companies. This is not a criticism, but it is important to acknowledge that school is not traditionally a safe place for students to be truly open, especially if they identify with a marginalized community, because being open means being vulnerable.

Sometimes young people have legitimate reasons to feel guarded and protect themselves. It is important to remember that the internet is not the culprit, any more than a house is dangerous because an abusive family member lives there. The safety issues in Open-Source Learning are the same as they are everywhere else; the key difference is in the way they are addressed, so that students feel valued and become empowered to express themselves and participate in solving their own problems.

Jeff, an internet-savvy student, celebrated Open-Source Learning at first. In his words, "this shows that school is finally catching up to the times." Jeff was smart, capable, and had something to contribute; he couldn't wait to apply his web design skills and get started.

But the days passed, and Jeff didn't build his blog or show any signs of curating his work anywhere online.

Jeff's teacher observed that something powerful must have happened to change Jeff's mind, and invited Jeff to a conversation—would Jeff trust Open-Source Learning enough to give the teacher a chance to understand him?

Fortunately, Jeff accepted and explained his position to the teacher. It turned out that Jeff had been bullied online the previous year, and as he got ready to go online, the trauma of the experience had returned: "I went through a lot, and I don't ever want to go through that again."

Jeff's teacher agreed that security was essential. He offered to collaborate on a security plan. They agreed on some basic ways to disguise Jeff's URL, protect access to his accounts with randomized passwords and two-party verification, and set up encrypted email and text clients. They also developed a contingency plan to archive Jeff's content so that he could move it quickly if he saw any indicator that his portfolio was hacked.

As soon as Jeff realized that he wouldn't have to look over his virtual shoulder, and he wouldn't have to defend himself against the teacher, he became the Most Valuable Programmer in the class. Jeff helped students launch their websites, taught them how to embed media and interactive widgets, and—most importantly—he provided a powerful reminder about how we all need to get our basic needs met so we feel free to do our best work.

In situations like this, teachers who assert their authority often cause more problems than they solve. Lecturing students about commitment and grades rarely leads to improved performance—more often, the student feels disregarded and either talks back or sulks.

By positioning students as valued colleagues and members of a network, Open-Source Learning levels the playing field. This does not diminish the teacher's standing in the student's eyes; in fact, it builds respect that is earned instead of demanded. Further, it invites—and sometimes challenges—students to articulate themselves in order to improve understanding and create relationships that can sustain confusion or disagreement.

Many teachers are excellent individual listeners who connect well with young people—on performance evaluations, administrators often describe this skill as "exceptional." Open-Source Learning bakes this into the model, so that asking questions, listening to answers, and acting to meet needs is no longer the exception. It is the rule.[4]

CRITICAL THINKING, PART ONE: SELECTING TOOLS FOR THE JOB

What is the best way for student to tell their stories? Is it a speech? A Haiku? A musical composition? A sculpture? A graphic novel? A performative dance? A meme?

One of the most telling decisions a learner can make is how best to represent the ideas they acquire, analyze, interpret, evaluate, synthesize, and put to use.

In the traditional classroom, teachers require all students to follow the same directions and complete the same assignment in the same way. This results in a batch of uniform posters, presentations, or papers.

In an Open-Source Learning environment, the medium of presentation represents yet another decision point, a chance to consider alternatives and provide evidence and reason in support of a best practice.

Selecting a tool requires understanding the tool, which in turn requires self-awareness and research. For an introductory list of resources that Open-Source Learning students have used, see page 149.

Which platform and media will you use to communicate?

CRITICAL THINKING, PART 2:
HOW TO ARGUE LIKE A CHAMPION

In Open-Source Learning, disagreement is healthy. Necessary, even. Argument isn't a competition to be won or lost; it is a search for the truth. We reason together to learn something new and come to understanding.

Disagreement is an essential part of learning. It is healthy for a person to push back and say, "No. That argument is totally wrong." In organizations, this is especially important—if you're not getting the benefit of everyone's thinking, you don't need them in the room.

One example of such constructive disagreement is the case of Thomas Hunter, who joined an Open-Source Learning class mid-year in 2011, after another teacher had labeled him with "an attitude problem."

Sure enough, on his first day in class, Thomas started an argument.

At the time, he had no idea what a syllogism was, but he constructed a neat deductive argument consisting of a major premise ("Everything I have ever been asked to do in an English class is completely irrelevant to my dream of becoming a professional videographer"), a minor premise ("This is an English class"), and a conclusion ("This is about to be another straight waste of my time").

Thomas didn't have all the information he needed to evaluate the truth of his premises, but based on his experiences, they were true enough, and his reasoning was valid—the conclusion followed from the premises.

Some of the other students rolled their eyes. They knew Thomas from other classes and they had seen this show before. They wanted the problem to go away so we could get back to what we were doing.

It didn't matter. Thomas nailed it and received the Student of the Week award.

He was speechless.

The gesture cost nothing. It was a token, and an investment; if a person has enough energy to argue, they have enough energy to do other things, things we hope will have a positive impact.

Thomas exceeded expectation. He embraced the true spirit of Open-Source Learning with so much energy that his projects have taken him around the world, positively impacted thousands of people, and started successful businesses that he continues to run (more on Thomas in the next chapter).

High-quality argument is a skill that requires communication and listening skills, critical thinking, and empathy. For Thomas to offer a cogent perspective in that moment, he had to have confidence in his knowledge, presence of mind to formulate a defensible position, and the commitment to defending his belief. I look for opportunities to lose arguments so that students can see how it is done; when that happens, I acknowledge learning something new and I thank the other person. We continue our relationship with our connection intact, and we know that if we disagree again, we will present our evidence and our reasoning and see what we see.

These conversations give us a chance to distinguish the qualities of ideas and experiences from our own preferences and opinions, and to investigate habits that hold us back from thinking more clearly, like suddenly cutting a conversation off by saying, "Well, you're entitled to your opinion."

Crimes Against Logic author Jamie Whyte asserts that none of us are entitled to our opinion:

"Does your right to your opinion oblige me to agree with you?" asked Whyte. "No—if only because that would be impossible to square with the universality of the right to an opinion."

"I, too, am entitled to the right to an opinion which might contradict yours," Whyte said. "Then we can't both do our duty toward each other. And think of the practical implications. Everyone would have to change his mind every time he met someone with a different opinion, changing his religion, his politics, his car, his eating habits."[5]

First of all, even though saying "I'm entitled to my opinion" is a cliché, that statement is a red herring. If we are arguing about, say, whether vanilla or chocolate ice cream is the best flavor, and someone says, "Well, fine, you're entitled to your opinion," they have effectively changed the topic and shut down the conversation. We are no longer exploring the truth of the ice cream matter.

We need to tap into the learning that people experience and value in real life. Open-Source Learning invites us to create and preserve connections with people and ways of communicating that speak to the real, practical, proven aspects of learning that make it so fun and important.

Chapter 5

The Power of the Network

If you want one year of prosperity, grow grain. If you want ten years of prosperity, grow trees.
  If you want one hundred years of prosperity, grow people.

Chinese proverb

If you want to go fast, go alone. If you want to go far, go with others.

African proverb[1]

Many professional organizations promote "the power of networking." Everyone has heard the saying, "It's not what you know, but who you know." But where in school do students learn how to build their network?

Open-Source Learning integrates the concept of an online network with a local learning community. Learners construct knowledge by

- building understandings between people
- analyzing communication techniques
- interpreting meaning
- evaluating logic
- making informed decisions that benefit them as individuals and participants in systems, which may include working groups, families, communities, organizations, cities, countries, or even the global population

In order to practice and refine their skills in all of these domains, students need to learn how to develop and maintain a healthy, productive network.

The classroom is too small and isolated of an environment to make network development meaningful. Using blogs and websites enables students to complement the in-class experience and connect it to the rest of the world.

Many teachers use online technology because they want to conserve paper and provide students with a way to access a course when they cannot attend in person. Some teachers discover that these tools can change the system in which we operate.

CASE STUDY: THE BRAIN WITH 200 LEGS

Science fiction author William Gibson gave an interview that appeared in *The Paris Review* and contained dozens of references and allusions.[2] More than one hundred students in several sections of an Open-Source Learning English course collaborated online to research, analyze, and document every element of the article in just a few hours.

The students were familiar with using social media to spontaneously organize videos and online challenges. They understood Howard Rheingold's concept of a smart mob:

"Smart mobs consist of people who are able to act in concert even if they don't know each other," wrote Rheingold. "The people who make up smart mobs cooperate in ways never before possible because they carry devices that possess both communication and computing capabilities."[3]

What would it take for everyone in the course to research, explain, and document every reference in the article—in one day?[4]

Students proposed curating their work with mind-mapping tools they found online. Here are three comments that represent the sentiments of the class (you can see more by following the link on p.150).

A.J.F.—I think that by using a mind map we can further develop our 200-leg brain. We will be able to see each other's thoughts, ideas, and opinions in real time. We will also be able to connect and relate our topics of discussion and form new ones as they come to mind through our current discussions.

Mari G.—A mind map allows us to create a network of imaginative ideas and join a cyberspace-like community that enhances our thinking, collaborating into one tree of thought.

Rachel V.—A mind map allows us to share more than just ideas. We can do that on a blog. A mind map instead allows a clearer way to connect ideas, and see other thought processes than our own. We have chains of thought, and are presented with new approaches that we may not have seen without the ability to connect ideas through a visual representation. This allows everyone to see how others think, which is rare. Everyone connects information differently. A mind map would enable people to understand conclusions, and understand the methods and processes used to reach the understanding that others who have collaborated may have.

A separate post asked students how they saw the working process.[5] The scope of their responses vividly demonstrated how the students proposed strategies. While some of their recommendations were different, the important thing is that the students begin with thoughtful reflection and clearly articulate their reasons. Practicing these skills enhances the decision-making quality of any organization, family, or community. (For more, please visit the original post online via the link in the end notes on p. 159.)

Kelly B.—Being a long interview, I believe we should split up into small groups or even individually examine each question and answer separately. Every group or person is assigned a different question in the interview. They, then, must research the different elements to the answer.

Mostly, we would search for the vocabulary we do not understand or more background on certain subjects the answer contains. Once all of the info was gathered, we would discuss the article as a whole with the knowledge we have. If we had any other questions about the research, we could then go back and edit each other's work if needed. It would be an individual effort ultimately grouped together as a team in the end.

Mariah C.—I agree with Kelly. Because of the length of this interview I think if we broke off into small groups and really focused on each question asked we will get better results. Having each group focus and research a specific question will be a lot more successful than doing it as a whole class.

If it was set up in groups we could really break down our assigned question, and research the vocabulary uses, underlying messages, and other facts that may support the answer. All in all, I think the most successful results in working with this interview is to break up into groups and then come together once everyone has gathered all of their information we can share our results as a class.

Carlos C.—I believe we should tackle this as a whole in order for all of us to have a sense of what is being discussed rather than one person knows something and the other knows something else. It keeps us together on what we know.

Jessica P.—I think that it is best that we start off working on this as one big group. This way it assures that everyone is at the same level with the text. After we have worked on it together for some time, we can then split off into smaller groups. Then all the groups can get together and share their information.

Alex D.—I believe we need to be assigned different tasks to maximize time efficiency. Sure, we can all study the same material and master it, but it would be much more time consuming. I have always been attracted to the idea of a "Jack of All Trades," and this can only be accomplished if people work as individuals or in small groups. Then after we have become masters in a particular topic, we can collaborate and share our newly developed ideas to be a part of something greater than ourselves.

The result was an online mind map that fully explicated an author's life and perspective on writing (for the results, see page 150).

Open-Source Learning engages participants and brings this sort of thinking to the surface, where it can simultaneously create value for each individual and the group as a whole. This is what it means to study in an "Academy of One"— each of us is completely autonomous in our thinking, and, by electing to work together, all of us become collaborative in sharing, refining, and coordinating our thinking to achieve goals together that would be impossible on our own.

The architecture of the internet is designed to connect people all over the world, all the time. Using tools that translate languages and media can supercharge our ability to form allegiances around ideas (as described in chapter 2). Open-Source Learning participants actively seek opportunities to form collaborative relationships that can co-exist within, between, or completely outside traditional organizational systems such as classes, grade levels, and schools.

Just as examining our belief systems can open our minds, and asking Big Questions can open new avenues of interdisciplinary exploration, creating an Open-Source Learning network opens communication channels with peers, experts, and others, both locally and around the world. It can also enrich conversation and understanding between people who are already connected through family, work, or school.

Any teacher can join an Open-Source Learning network or start one of their own. Even if your school does not support Open-Source Learning, or if you are navigating a teaching culture that is ensnared in hidebound tradition, you can still create an online network to amplify and accelerate learning. All you need is a reason, some people who share that reason or have their own, and access to the internet, and you are ready to go. Set up a blog or a website that invites readers to share your learning journey, and create links on that site to the other members of your network. If you are new to blogging, or learning online, see the resources on page 150.

If you are teaching a school course, create a course blog that includes a page with a directory of Member Blogs. If you are a student in the course, you can do this just as easily—and, since taking this sort of initiative isn't assumed to be part of your "job," it establishes you as a leader and adds the value of information and inspiration for others. It's a revolutionary act that helps all and hurts no one.

On the Member Blogs directory, everyone in the network—and people from outside the classroom and the school—can see everyone else's blog. Reading individual blogs provides insight into each person's content and thinking, as well as critical thinking, design choices, metadata, and even personality. Reading many blogs provides comparative analysis that may be used to refine and enhance both the core academic program and creative extensions such as Big Questions.

Since anyone in the network can share their blogs with everyone from whom they want to learn, students are empowered to form communities of interest, support, and critique.

The power of the Open-Source Learning network resides in how it is used, and the effects it creates as experienced by its members—and also in what it is *not*.

THE OPEN-SOURCE LEARNING NETWORK:
WHAT IT IS, AND WHAT IT IS NOT

Sometimes the most effective way to be clear and specific in school is to draw a contrast. This is important when it comes to the language of Open-Source Learning networks, because people tend to substitute and conflate familiar words for "groups of learners," and that dilutes meaning.

Let's first define the Open-Source Learning network by stating what it is *not*.

An Open-Source Learning network is not a school, a course, or a class. These terms and the concepts to which they refer are symbolic of a traditional belief system in which school organization and curriculum is designed, pre-packaged, and imposed by hierarchical authority figures as a matter of policy.

A *class* exists in theoretical form. People are directed to a specific place and time based on school programs and schedules.

A class does not have to produce anything or even function well to be considered a class. The class is designated to "meet" whether or not anyone actually shows up.

A *course* also exists in theoretical form. It has a title, a description, and a syllabus, whether or not anyone ever meets as a class to study it.

An Open-Source Learning network, on the other hand, does not exist until the moment learners bring it into existence through agreement and action. Learners co-create the entire experience, including the process, the content, and the community structure. Each network is unlike any other network because it is a unique combination of people at a unique moment in time. It only functions to the extent that its connections are strengthened by members who share information.

The learners who participate in Open-Source Learning are more than students. In school, students are defined in passive relationship to a teacher—they are taught. Learners establish interdependent relationships and actively engage with information and tools that accelerate their understanding and amplify their self-expression.

These distinctions are meaningful. If we want to increase understanding and productivity, then our language should clarify and illuminate. It becomes important to use specific terms that accurately reflect the dynamic of Open-Source Learning instead of traditional education industry jargon.

Language is a powerful influence on our thinking and how we see the world: it can be an oppressive tool for enforcing conformity, or it can be a liberating way to explore the shared value of possibility.

The language of education is unclear—so unclear, in fact, that it confounds experts. Tom Gruber was co-founder, chief technology officer, and head of design for the team that created the Siri virtual assistant now used in the Apple operating system. Gruber spent years studying language, management, and the terms that people and organizations use to delegate tasks and coordinate projects.

Gruber's work in artificial intelligence focuses on how machines can interpret our intent through language to help us get things done. He is an expert in using semantics to optimize performance.

After being asked to evaluate how well the language of school helps educators and learners get things done, and spending an hour trying to parse some of the terms used in education policy and school management, Gruber closed his eyes hard and pinched the top of his nose with his thumb and forefinger. "I don't know," he said, "This all sounds like a bunch of word salad."[6]

There may be another purpose to the language of school. As science fiction author Philip K. Dick put it: "The basic tool for the manipulation of reality is the manipulation of words. If you can control the meaning of words, you can control the people who must use them."[7]

School has a bizarre lexicon that does not make sense anywhere else; no wonder Gruber was so befuddled. Rather than providing clarity or shared meaning, its primary function seems to be reinforcing cultural authority on campus.

Consider the word *tardy*, for example, which sounds so petty and annoying that using it actually makes the person who uses it sound like a petty and annoying person, particularly if that person uses it outside of a school attendance office or a parent teacher conference. Imagine a strategic planning meeting at a tech startup:

"Hey Michelle, we were supposed to get started four minutes ago. How come you're tardy?"

"There was traffic, Josh. Why are you talking like my third-grade teacher?"

The same holds true for many words, terms, and phrases that are used in school and nowhere else. Even the words *student* and *teacher* are so loaded with meaning that they lock people into roles and specific patterns of behavior.

In an Open-Source Learning environment, students and teachers are *members of the network*. Apart from the term being an accurate descriptor, it's cool. We want to experience a sense of belonging in a desirable system.

Being a member of an Open-Source Learning network appeals to students because the perks of the network include the exciting aspects of culture that exist outside of school, where computers and people connect to create synergies and great ideas.

The members make the network. Every Open-Source Learning experience is brought into existence and documented as a function of applied free will and collaborative decision-making in action.

As Terry Lawless, keyboardist from the band U2, said to members of an Open-Source Learning network when he visited their class, "To me there's nothing like creation. What's the highest power anyone can think of? The Creator. If you can bring that down to your level and make something . . . it doesn't matter if you're a cabinet maker, if you're an artist, if you're a writer, or if you're a musician, you create something where nothing was before. That is your legacy and you will live forever that way."[8]

Making decisions and creating something tangible and functional is an expression of understanding, and also of power. Each individual in an Open-Source Learning network has the authority to engage and act. The members are also the owners. In the network, the teacher may be a "first among equals" who guides and supports the process, but the network's integrity depends on everyone's open communication and mutual respect.

The importance of each member's contribution to the network brings us back to Open-Source Learning's integration with digital culture and the "peer-to-peer" structure of the internet. This is a departure from the traditional "one-to-many" model of classroom communication, in which the teacher has the authority to communicate at will to however many students there are in a classroom, but students must follow rules that prevent peer-to-peer communication and unsolicited feedback.

Traditional school norms are based on a specific belief system, which in turn is based on a series of assumptions. For example, we assume that if students are free to speak at will, the entire class will be noisy, and the teacher will lose control—therefore, a "good" teacher controls the students and forces them into silence.

To maintain the order of the one-to-many broadcast, educators spend millions on conferences, books, and software—just to learn strategies for getting students to be quiet and follow instructions in an orderly fashion.

At the same time, however, a "good" teacher will also elicit "student participation" on demand. When administrators evaluate teachers, they often comment on how well the teacher keeps student quiet *and* gets students to participate when called upon.

Passive student participation-on-demand is characteristic of a systemic culture that Brazilian educator Paolo Freire described as the "banking" model of education. Freire observed that in this culture, "The scope of action allowed to the students extends only as far as receiving, filing, and storing the deposits."

"But in the last analysis," Freire wrote, "it is the people themselves who are filed away through the lack of creativity, transformation, and knowledge in this (at best) misguided system."[9]

The product of a one-to-many broadcast is not the "community of lifelong learners" that so many schools promise—it is an audience that is trained to sit still. This communication structure is similar to watching television, only worse. When we watch TV, we may want to yell at the people on the screen, but we know they cannot see or hear us. It can be frustrating but there is no getting around the technological limitation. In fact, sometimes knowing that no one can hear you can be a liberating experience. From the comfort of your own couch, you can yell at athletes or movie characters all you want without getting shushed or kicked out.

The structure and practice of the one-to-many broadcast reinforces the belief that the authority figure at the front of the room knows everything, including when to let others contribute, and the rest of the audience knows nothing.

No wonder that so many students come away from school thinking that they are "bad" at a particular subject or skill. The broader, long-term implication—that the vast majority of people should keep their mouths shut, that their ideas are less important or valuable because they do not have hierarchical authority—proves disastrous for nurturing precisely the type of independent inquiry and innovative thinking that the education system is supposedly intended to encourage. How can graduates of obedience school be expected to assert themselves in a democratic government or a competitive marketplace?

The relationship between instructor and students in the Open-Source Learning process is much more productive. The teacher serves the learning community as a first among equals. Not only does this model give learners the opportunity to co-construct experiences and knowledge—which requires them to think critically and creatively—but it also inspires a healthy, well-deserved sense of respect for all.

HOW THE OPEN-SOURCE LEARNING NETWORK OPERATES

The key to constructively disrupting the one-to-many broadcast is opening channels for documenting and sharing all of the thinking that is happening in the network at any given time.

In school, the one-to-many broadcast is so dominant that it is difficult to imagine a large group learning in any other way. To prevent interrupting the flow of the main source of information, we cut off feedback loops and multimodal interaction between peers and the outside world.

The main purpose of Open-Source Learning is to support students as *active learners*. It is entirely feasible to create opportunities for reflection, self-expression, analysis, evaluation, debate, remixing information, and sharing with the outside world, all without disrupting the speaker.

Open-Source Learning teachers do this in a variety of ways in K-12 classrooms, often by using multiple computers and screens.

For example, a high school teacher set up her classroom with a laptop plugged into a cable that feeds the ceiling-mounted projector and displays images on a large screen at the front of the room. She used a screen mode that allows her to see a different screen on the laptop itself; attendance, school email, and other administrative features appear on the laptop screen, while the students around the room see only the course blog and related images on the large wall-mounted screen.

She uses second laptop for social media and streaming music that plays while students write in their journals, a word processor she uses to compose blog posts and ideas for future writing assignments, and an internet browser to research ideas and update the course blog. She usually has two or three browser windows open at a time, with thirty to forty open tabs of research, current events, and primary source materials in each.

If she has access to an additional screen, she uses it to project hashtag-based "Twitter falls" and etherpads or Google documents that everyone around the room can use to make real-time comments, ask questions, brainstorm, and post memes, jokes, or whatever else they associate with the ideas of the moment.

Open-Source Learning networks that operate in this sort of environment are more highly interactive than traditional classrooms. Members of the network are more communicative with one another, and more interdependent, and therefore they are more aware of how other members interact.

In this environment, performance evaluation becomes a function of interaction with multiple people, rather than test scores or letter grades on assignments. This will be the focus of chapter 6.

Chapter 6

Every Day Is Judgment Day

Organization can never be a substitute for initiative and for judgment.

Louis D. Brandeis[1]

Politicians use statistics in the same way that a drunk uses lampposts—
for support rather than illumination.

Andrew Lang[2]

An Open-Source Learning teacher chided a top-performing student about the pace of her online publishing. The teacher knew that the student was in the middle of research, but wanted to remind her, in the presence of other students, that others wanted to see her thinking and her progress.

"It's been a week since I've seen you post anything," the teacher said. "Did they turn the internet off on your street? Were you trapped under something heavy?"

She smiled and said, "Don't you judge me!"

Don't you judge me.

That phrase has become a parody of itself. *Don't you judge me* can be funny when it is meant to be, but its literal intent is rooted in a post-Jerry Springer culture where people who should absolutely feel ashamed of their behavior no longer do, and instead brazenly attempt to make their problems our problems.

As author James Twitchell wrote in his book *For Shame: The Loss of Common Decency in American Culture*, "Instead of viewing shame as a powerful socializing device, we see it as a hindrance to individual fulfillment."[3]

Shame has largely disappeared from social contact. When was the last time a public figure showed genuine remorse for something they really wished they had done differently? The Houston Astros were caught cheating during the World Series, and not a single one of them offered a believable apology.[4]

The lack of consensus about morality has created a great deal of confusion in our culture: Do the ends justify the means? Is it wrong if you don't get caught? If everyone else cheats, how can I win? What is a meritocracy anyway?

Open-Source Learning takes the concept of merit literally and seriously. We aim for excellence and we believe we can do better.

To those who would tell us not to judge you, please be clear on this point: *Of course we're going to judge you.*

THE BREAKFAST BURRITO PRINCIPLE

In front of you are two breakfast burritos. One burrito was prepared by the loving hands of the most talented chef you can imagine. It is piping hot. Steam rises from the soft flour tortilla that embraces fresh cubed Yukon gold potatoes, eggs from happy, local pastured hens, green chiles, and fresh cilantro from the garden.

The other burrito was processed two years ago by a frozen food company that took over a converted auto parts factory next to a waste water treatment plant. It smells like freezer. It has been frozen, thawed, and frozen again, then microwaved. The hardened ends are warm, but you can still see ice crystals in the middle. This burrito has blue spots and is hairy with mold.

You get to choose one burrito.

Are you ready to judge now? It is essential for you to make some sort of choice here. If you make the right choice, you get to enjoy breakfast. If you make the wrong choice, you alert your network that you don't know any better, and hopefully they will help educate you.

Judging—being able to evaluate what is of quality and what is good for us—is not only advantageous but essential to our survival.

Discernment helps us make decisions that range from shopping to ethics to social relationships. We have to be able to judge quality. If you cannot tell what is good for you from what isn't, you are going to get sick and die sooner than the rest of us.

How does judgment enter into evaluating our learning and our teaching? How do we know what we know?

The data generated through Open-Source Learning provides a rich alternative to testing. The original content and metadata that learners produce provides insight into what they are thinking and how they are thinking about it. We can benchmark strengths and identify opportunities for improvement, so that graduates have a portfolio of knowledge and skill, and—far more importantly—so that they can recognize when they have a need to learn and execute on a strategy that will meet their needs.

Standardized testing offers none of that. So why do schools spend so much time, energy, and money on testing? Understanding this part of the education belief system requires some historical context.

PASSING THE TEST

Some tests serve a valid purpose in learning; they can reveal a learners' strengths and needs for improvement. In a formative test, the learner performs a task which can be analyzed in order to refine a course of study and practice that acknowledges and validates areas of strength, corrects errors, and addresses areas of deficiency.

Over time, however, three social beliefs have combined to hijack the value of testing and turn it into a profitable theater of the grotesque: racism, championing science without understanding science, and meritocracy.

In 1904, Alfred Binet, director of the Psychology Department at the Sorbonne, was commissioned by the French minister of education to develop an assessment instrument that could be given to students who performed poorly in school, for the purpose of identifying those students who needed additional support or special education.

Binet designed his test specifically to help students grow and improve, not to label them. The scale he developed in 1908 took students through a series of tasks that began with tasks appropriate for younger ages and proceeded to get more difficult. The age associated with the last tasks a student could complete became the student's "mental age" and was subtracted from their chronological age to generate their test score.[5]

A few years after Binet died, German psychologist William Stern proposed dividing the mental age by the chronological age; this is how the test became known as the Intelligence Quotient (IQ) test.

The IQ test was popularized in America by Lewis Terman, a Stanford professor who believed that the test score was a symbol of general intelligence that in turn was an innate, inherited quality. Unlike Binet, who wanted to help every learner, Terman's purpose for using the test was to sort people by intelligence. High IQ people could become professionals; low IQ people were to be removed from society.[6] Considering that Terman believed intelligence to be inherited and that his doctoral dissertation defended his own intelligence tests by using racial and national stereotypes, it is reasonable to conclude that he was using Binet's test to justify segregation and eugenics.

Nevertheless, Terman's efforts were successful. The Stanford-Binet IQ Test became the standard for intelligence testing. It was used to label, limit, and exclude students—not to help them with unique needs that were challenging their ability to be successful, as Binet originally intended.

The evolution of standardized testing as a punitive, exclusionary practice continued with applications in the military and higher education. One of Terman's collaborators in advocating for widespread testing was Robert Yerkes, a Harvard professor who wanted to establish psychology as a quantitative, natural science. Like many of today's academics and policy makers, Yerkes associated science with rigor, and rigor with numbers and quantification. For these reasons, mental testing made sense; it could generate the data that would lend his profession the credibility he sought.

Yerkes successfully lobbied for the army "Alpha" and "Beta" tests, which were administered to nearly 2 million recruits during World War I.[7] Whatever influence these tests did or did not have in the military (there is no evidence that the tests correlated with performance in the field), they did generate data. Yerkes used this work to create a brand of perceived credibility ("Army tested!") and promote testing everyone in every walk of life.

So began the era of mass testing.

World War I produced many technological advancements that helped soldiers fight and kill. But the tool that emerged from the conflict that may have had the most devastating, long-lasting impact on social policy is the multiple-choice exam.

As Stephen Jay Gould notes in his book, *The Mismeasure of Man*, "The major impact of the tests did not fall upon the army. Yerkes may not have brought the army its victory, but he had won his battle. He now had uniform data on 1.75 million men, and he had devised, in the Alpha and Beta exam, the first mass produced written tests of intelligence."[8]

Today, most of the multiple-choice exams that teachers give are criterion-referenced tests. Questions are set against a structured curriculum and intended to measure student retention and understanding. Criterion-referenced tests can be used as formative evaluations. Students are sometimes shown their results, along with information that will help them improve where they answered items incorrectly. The general purpose for this type of test is to give the student and the teacher an idea of how well the student has mastered concepts or skills in order to support learning. Sometimes criterion-referenced tests are given before and after a lesson, or multiple times for the sake of practice and improvement.

Standardized tests are norm-referenced tests. Items on these exams test a wide range of concepts and skills, and scores are analyzed and interpreted relative to other individuals or groups.

Some classroom tests can be norm-referenced, if for example, they are graded on a curve. Standardized tests are generally summative evaluations. Norm-referenced tests are used to sort students by performance level, or to label populations of students in order to program coursework, or to allocate or restrict funding. Students are not given individual feedback about how they might use the results to improve, and they do not usually have a second chance to take the test for a better score.

A careful examination of an answer sheet to a multiple-choice test tells us very little. In fact, the only thing we really know is which answers the respondent bubbled in. We have no idea why. Were they confident in the correct answer? Were they guessing? Were they confident in the *incorrect* answer? Were they entertaining themselves by making a pattern with the bubbles or answering "C" all the way down the column?

Looking at questions like this has been a gold mine of intuition about what's wrong with education. For example, problems with multiple-choice testing were a focus of Professor James Bruno of the UCLA Graduate School of Education and Information Studies. Bruno's engineering background and research experience at the Rand Corporation, coupled with his extensive research in education policy, statistical modeling, computer programming, and teacher training, led him to conclude that one-dimensional multiple-choice testing was a colossal waste of time.

"Multiple-choice data is garbage," Jim once fumed as he combed through data from the Los Angeles Unified School District in his office. "Who can tell if these students are brilliant, well-informed, or just magna cum lucky?"[9]

Bruno developed an instrument called the Information-Referenced Test (IRT) to provide insight on what he called the "second dimension" of testing: the respondent's reason for answering a question in a particular way. The questions on the IRT could be related to any topic or course, and they might even be worded like traditional multiple-choice questions.

The difference was in the answer options. Instead of A, B, C, and D, the Information-Referenced Test offered A through M, with a variety of options for gaining credit for answers.

In the courses where Bruno administered the IRT, students took the test both ways: traditional multiple-choice scoring with three answer options per item, and the IRT scoring with twelve answer options per item. All students scored higher on the IRT. They reported that they felt like the test was more closely aligned with documenting and improving their learning experience. The data showed where students were informed, uninformed, and misinformed, and also showed where instruction could be improved.

Unfortunately, two-dimensional testing is not commonly used in schools. Traditional multiple-choice formats and standardized testing practices *that have nothing to do with student learning* have maintained a stranglehold on education policy for three reasons:

1) We still have a cultural bias that suggests numbers are scientific. Testing data is easy to count and appears easy to interpret and describe, so people who know very little about student learning or classroom instruction can sound knowledgeable about both.
2) Everyone who has passed a test believes in the test. Every teacher and every administrator was rewarded by that system. Successful people love to believe in meritocracy, the idea that they succeeded because of their talent, or their determination, or some other personal quality that earned, deserved—merited—their success. It is psychologically painful to admit the alternative.
3) Any alternative to existing policy will have to be more than a good idea—it must be a campaign, funded and designed to succeed in the arenas of marketing and lobbying against publishers and testing companies who seek to limit competition.

Open-Source Learning emphasizes the intentional use of tools to help learners succeed. This critique of multiple-choice testing raises a question: What are we measuring, and with what tools?

DRASTIC TIMES, DRASTIC MEASURES

Modern Times, Modern Measures

It's a cruel irony. When it comes to learning, school as an institution is very limited in its approaches to evaluating performance. We would do well to consider how other social institutions that are obsessed with tradition and statistics have adapted.

For decades, most baseball fans—especially kids—knew the major leaguers' key statistics: batting averages, stolen bases, hits, runs batted in, earned run averages, stolen bases.

Over time, however, we developed different ways of looking at the game and analyzing the value of a player's contributions. Team managers and front-office leadership started using computers to compile and model the statistics that most influence the outcomes of games, and everyone realized that the old ways, while still meaningful, did not tell the whole story.

For example, a player's batting average is the number of times the player gets a hit divided by the number of times a player gets a chance to bat. However, there are other ways to get on base, such as getting hit by a pitch, reaching base on an error, and walking on four balls outside the strike zone. These plays and others are ways for a player to be productive and help the team without actually getting a hit, and none of them are accounted for in the traditional batting average statistic.

Statisticians created new ways of looking at batters' performance, such as on base percentage and slugging percentage, which takes different kinds of hits into account.

In fact, the Society for American Baseball Research, which is known as SABR, has done so much work in this regard that it spawned a new field known as Sabermetrics.[10]

Sabermetrics has created new ways of describing and modeling player contributions to their teams, brand-new statistics based on multivariate equations with fancy names, like Wins Above Replacement (WAR) and Value Over Replacement Player (VORP). Both of these statistics use multiple performance statistics to create a model for the value of a player to a team.

The application of these statistics got people's attention. The Oakland A's famously entered the 2002 season without star players from the year before and a payroll about one-third the size of the New York Yankees. Billy Beane, Oakland's general manager, used Sabermetrics so successfully that the A's finished first in their division and won twenty games in a row. The season made an impact on popular culture; it was memorialized in a book by Michael Lewis titled *Moneyball*, which in turn was made into a movie starring Brad Pitt.

The perception that data analysis and statistical modeling could lead to success made the practice compelling, which made it more acceptable for others to adopt. Traditional statistics such as batting average and runs scored are still viable measure of performance, but newer metrics play an increasingly important role in management and performance in baseball. Theo Epstein, as general manager with the Boston Red Sox and Chicago Cubs, used Sabermetrics to help end two of the longest World Series Championship droughts (86 years and 108 years, respectively) in baseball history.

The moral of the story here has little to do with collecting or analyzing things we can count. It's the fact that there are many ways to expand the conversation about quantifiable data as a signal of intangible qualities. Most importantly, it's important to remember that the conversation isn't really about the data at all. What matters most is what we do with the information that we gather and analyze. In the fifteen years following that 2002 season, the Oakland A's finished last or second-to-last in their division almost as often as they finished first.

* * *

Sacrificing the sacred cows of traditional statistics has expanded beyond baseball, with special implications for individuals who work in collaborative systems.

Shane Battier was considered an average professional basketball player. He had excelled in high school and college, but in the NBA everyone thought his reputation exceeded his ability. A *New York Times Magazine* article by Michael Lewis (the *Moneyball* author) described Battier this way: "Here we have a basketball mystery: a player is widely regarded inside the NBA as, at best, a replaceable cog in a machine driven by superstars. And yet every team he has every played on has acquired some magical ability to win."[11]

Traditional basketball statistics—points, rebounds, field goal percentage, free throw percentage, blocks, steals, and fouls, to name a few—are measures of individual achievements. Focusing on these measurements creates a conflict. Unlike baseball, where a player who plays well as an individual almost always helps the team, a basketball player can help himself and hurt his team at the same time.

In professional basketball, where players are paid based in large part on their individual statistics, every decision on the court can be maximized to the player's advantage and the team's detriment. Even assists—the passes that lead to baskets—can be accumulated to benefit a player's personal statistics at the expense of easy baskets or other plays that would more likely lead to a basket or a team victory. A lot of NBA players who are called "franchise players" are actually superstars whose individual performances are presumed to make their teams more competitive.

Battier, on the other hand, was so good at making the players around him better, so good at reading the flow of the game and blending in, that he influenced the outcome of games while being invisible on the traditional "stat sheet." He would know the tendencies of opposing players well enough to force them into situations where they were less effective. He would understand his team's offense so well that he would dilute the opposing team's defense. He even asked to not start a game so that he could guard the other team's best scorer later in the game.

There is no statistic for that.

Seeing a professional athlete make such selfless decisions raises an interesting question about learning and education. If we want learners to graduate with skills that help them connect and collaborate with others, why aren't learners evaluated on the things they do that help others succeed?

Students do things every day that do not get recorded in their academic records: you help a classmate with their homework. You ask the question in class that everyone secretly wanted to ask because the teacher's explanation made no sense. These actions are important—they help you learn and they help the people around you learn. People see your efforts and benefit directly from them. But doing all of this doesn't help your GPA

We can create an environment where network members leverage the community structure outlined in chapter 5 to reflect and provide feedback, so that assessment and evaluation are integrated with learning in ways that strengthen each practice and support expansive sharing outside the network.

CASES: THE MIRROR AND THE 5PH1NX

Open-Source Learning requires students to reflect on their own thinking and their own effort, so that they can learn in an honest way, without trying to con or impress anyone, in order to succeed in a variety of fields and tasks. Students must be able to evaluate themselves, and participate in "360-degree reviews," which are far more effective when they are conducted in a collegial, timely fashion.

1. The Mirror

In Open-Source Learning courses, students reflect on their thought processes, work habits, and performance. Through the use of daily journals and formal periodic self-assessments, students develop their ability to understand and articulate the connection between their thinking and their work product. At the end of every progress reporting period, students answer the following questions:

• Describe something you did really well in this course over the past month. What strengths did this demonstrate?

- Describe something in this course that you would have liked to do better. What will you need to improve in order to feel confident about your work in this area?
- Are you confident that the amount of effort you put into your learning is supporting your success? Have you established the routines you need to achieve your goals?
- At this point in the semester, what letter grade do you deserve? Why? Is this aligned with the goal you set for yourself at the beginning of the semester? What grade are you aiming for on the semester report card?

These and similar, related questions create conversations and online documents that in turn serve as benchmarks for students to set goals and reflect. They may also be asked in a personal interview, which other students may attend and document to provide feedback.

2. 5PH1NX

On a Monday morning, students in three English classes discovered anomalies in the day's entries on their course blog. The date was wrong. Some of the letters were in a slightly different color. The journal topic for the day was:

> "In The Principles of Psychology (1890), William James wrote, 'The faculty of voluntarily bringing back a wandering attention, over and over again, is the very root of judgment, character, and will. No one is compose sui if he have it not. An education which should improve this faculty would be the education par excellence.' How have your experiences in this course helped you focus your attention? What do you still need to work on? What elements of the following text (from Haruki Murakami's *1Q84*) draw your attention and help you construct meaning?"

The selection from *1Q84* that followed was dialogue from a mysterious exchange between two people that intimated that things are not what they seem.

Adding to the strangeness, some of the letters were bright blue instead of black. Students who paid close attention realized that the letters themselves formed a pattern:

Find the jokers.

The jokers were real playing cards that were placed by the teacher around the classroom and in students' journals. This was yet another unexpected call to adventure.

Although they didn't know it yet, students were playing the liminal role of Oedipus trying to solve the riddle of the Sphinx in order to usher out an old way of thinking and introduce the new. Except that now, 5PH1NX was spelled in leetspeak, an internet style of typing that replaces letters with similar-looking numbers or symbols, and served as an acronym for, "Student Peer Heuristic for Information Exchange."

The old way. An authority figure sets the rules, packages the information for a passive audience, and unilaterally evaluates each learner's performance.

The new way. In Open-Source Learning the learner pursues a path of inquiry within communities that function as end-to-end user networks. Each individual begins learning with a question and pursues answers through an interdisciplinary course of study that emphasizes multiple modalities. Learners collaborate with mentors and receive feedback from experts, community-based peers, and the public. They are the heroes of learning journeys.

Heroes don't respond to syllabi. They respond to calls to adventure.

The Open-Source Learning environment had prepared students for the unforeseen. By the time students met the 5PH1NX, they had learned about habits of mind, operating schema, digital culture and community, self-expression, collaboration, free play, autonomy, confidence/trust/risk, and resilience. These ideas had been reinforced through nonfiction articles and literary selections such as Montaigne's *Essays*, Plato's *Allegory of the Cave*, Bukowski's *Laughing Heart*, Shakespeare's *Hamlet*, Sartre's *No Exit* and others.

The first poem assigned in that course was Bukowski's "Laughing Heart": *The Gods will give you chances. Know them. Take them.* This has implications far beyond the classroom. In today's world, we are presented with an overwhelming quantity and variety of data in our physical and virtual lives; to cope, we must improve the ways we seek, select, curate, analyze, evaluate, and act on information.

On the back of each joker card was a QR code that linked to a blog page with riddles and clues to a search. At this point, most students realized they were playing a game. But after a second set of quests on campus and online, students noticed a shift in 5PH1NX.

A couple of weeks after the first clue was posted, during a seminar on Derrida's concept of Free Play, a student said, "We learn best when adults take away the crutches and there is no safety net." The quote was used in the next clue; students realized that the game was not pre-determined. 5PH1NX was evolving in response to their contributions.

The student's comment led to the creation of "Feats of Wisdom" that engaged learners over Spring Break in fun, collaborative, social media-friendly missions that required engagement in the community, expansion of their personal learning networks, and documentation on their blogs. Students completed straightforward academic tasks, but they also submitted entries with videos of colleagues ordering hamburgers in old English, writing essays underwater and on roller coasters, interviewed people in the community about vocabulary words, and recited "To be or not to be" from memory in public places.

A page on the Feats of Wisdom blog entitled "Identifying and Rewarding Greatness" invited them to share stories about these adventures:

"If you see something that was done with love, that pushed the boundaries, set the standard, broke the mold, pushed the envelope, raised the bar, blew the doors off, or rocked in some previously unspecified way, please bring it to the attention of the group by posting a link to it in a comment here."

The students did something more effective. They started building. One student hacked the entire game and created her own online version. Other students analyzed the implications for identifying and rewarding greatness. They concluded that one teacher could not possibly observe how ninety-six students were working over vacation out in the community and online to accomplish the Feats of Wisdom, and created a site where students could share their accomplishments and claim credit.

Students applied the same logic to learning and coursework in general. After all, even the most engaged, conscientious teacher only sees a student a few hours each week in artificially controlled conditions. The learner presumably spends their whole life in the company of their own mind. Who is more qualified to report on the learner's thinking?

With these thoughts in mind, students created "Project Infinity," a peer-to-peer assessment platform through which students could independently assign value to those thoughts and activities they deemed worthy. Because the 5PH1NX experience was a three-week exercise in gamification, Project Infinity quickly expanded to include Big Questions and other elements of coursework.

This was learner-centered assessment in action. Learners identified a need and an opportunity, they built a tool for the purpose, they managed it themselves, and they used it in a meaningful way to support each other's achievement in all aspects of learning, including the traditional core curriculum.

IMPLICATIONS

Assessment (and its purposeful use) plays an important role in Open-Source Learning. It is an important connection between learning communities and other social systems. In addition to evaluating understanding or skill, the processes of giving, receiving, and applying constructive critique makes learners better thinkers, innovators, motivators, collaborators, coworkers, friends, relatives, spouses, teammates, and neighbors.

More often than not, the feedback learners receive and value in their everyday lives comes from peers, not authority figures. Helping students become better at both delivering and acting on feedback from peers is essential to their success beyond the classroom.

But implementing peer-based assessment can be problematic in educational institutions where *evaluative* authority is traditionally conflated with *hierarchical* authority, and where economic and political influences have focused attention on summative, quantitative, standardized measurement.

Pursuing an interdisciplinary path of inquiry in an interest-based community brings learners closer to understanding their own habits of mind and gives them practice in the culture they will be expected to join when they graduate.

Students get to see and be seen. They develop their capacities for collaboration, delegation, facilitating conversations, and other highly valued skills in plain view, where peers, experts, and the public can join, critique, and validate them. Students come to understand how others see their work. They begin to take pride in their efforts and they decide where to invest their time and energy. Toward the end of each academic year, they present their learning—and themselves—as a masterpiece.

As one Open-Source Learning student wrote at the end of a school year, "A constant theme I noticed while watching the masterpiece presentations was a sense of pride. Everyone was pleased with what they had accomplished. No one was happy to be done; they were happy to show what they had done and many, including my group, are continuing with our masterpieces because it is something we are *proud* of. It is a great feeling to show something that you can look at and say 'Yeah, I did that and I'm proud of it.'"

"I noticed pride in my group's masterpiece. A couple people in my group wanted to go into business and I wanted to go in cosmetology, so I was able to incorporate what I was passionate about in the masterpiece. Allyson was very proud to show everyone her pictures from her summer program in Michigan where they learned all about genetics and got a hands-on experience with a professor. Jose showed us about his football career and how he wants to motivate people to do better. Ashley and Bianca are really into comics and showed us some of their work. Edmond wants to be a writer and he was able to show us a little bit of the book he has been writing."

Open-Source Learning produces far more quantitative and qualitative data than testing does. Each year, students create millions of discrete digital artifacts including instant messages and texts, emails, social media posts, blog posts, comments, and others. Even their pen-and-paper work can be scanned and uploaded.

Artifacts that can be shared are more valuable than artifacts that cannot be shared. Consider the test or the essay in a traditional, closed-system learning environment. Students write essays. The teacher—one person—reads them. The teacher grades the papers and returns them to the class, who then unanimously dispose of the work. The entire transaction is private. How can anyone else value them at all? How can students stand beside their work and be seen for what they do?

In a traditional closed system, they can't. Whatever value students perceive is usually associated with the grade; maybe they read the teacher's comments and suggestions. Then, they stuff the papers into the bottom of backpacks, eventually to be thrown away. The end result: the work is never shared, and it's lost to history, whether it was brilliant or desperately in need of improvement.

However, when students upload that same essay to their blogs, they can still get constructive feedback from the teacher, *and* they also get constructive feedback from everyone who follows their blogs and from everyone with whom they share the work. Over time, the essays remain available to review, analyze, and compare along with the rest of their work, along with all of the work from colleagues in their Open-Source Learning network.

We can also analyze and interpret digital artifacts in many other ways. Apart from metrics like word counts and due dates, we can create content analyses and graphically represent ideas with tools such as word clouds.

We can also review metadata. This is the data that provides information about the content that a learner publishes. Sometimes the data about when a student posts, how often, or the volume of posts and comments on a blog tell a story or raise a question. For instance, a track star and straight-A student consistently posted her best work around 2:30 a.m. This raised a question about sleep and health, which she answered this way: "After school and practice I feel tapped and all I want to do is eat dinner, relax for a little while, and go to sleep. My grades are my priority, so I try to get to bed by 7:30 or 8:00 P.M. so I can wake up at 2:00 A.M. and get my work done when I feel alert."

Metadata can also be used in reflective practice to help learners identify patterns in their habits and correlations with the quality of their work product.

As we know in the working world, some people are early birds, some people work best on the vampire shift, some plan meticulously in advance, and some treat the deadline as their driving force.

Open-Source Learning data can also be used to evaluate network dynamics such as engagement. When teachers take attendance, they are just counting bodies—who knows whether a student is paying attention on a given day? Websites, on the other hand, measure all sorts of behavior. Some of the data is coarse and needs further analysis. Consider a teacher who teaches approximately 170 high school students in two courses. The two course blogs receive an average of 4,000 and 13,000 page views each month. That translates into about 100 page views per person *per day*. This demonstrates engagement and invites further inquiry.

Most educators are not website experts, and understanding the user experience is a full-time job, so a logical next step in the evolution of Open-Source Learning would be for schools or third parties to analyze and support learner-focused websites with research on the user experience. Conducting further research would provide insight on current use and suggest refinements to support learners' needs.

While Open-Source Learning naturally creates opportunities for collaboration and mentorship, it also champions self-sufficiency. There are many ways for teachers and learners to conduct their own research on users without making any requests of anyone else. Doing this work and posting about it creates value for the person who runs the site, the people who use the site, and anyone who reads about the improvement process.

To help you get started, the Digital Communications Division in the United States Department of Health and Human Services has created a website dedicated to usability[12] and encourages distribution of its content in the public domain. Research methods listed on the site include

- Card Sorting, which can help design or evaluate the information architecture of a site, including what to put on the homepage, labels, and navigation;
- Focus Groups and Individual Interviews, in which users participate in discussions about their attitudes, habits, and needs;
- Expert Review, in which experienced colleagues in education and/or usability benchmark the site against best practices and guidelines;

These strategies and many others are fairly easy to implement, and they represent the next level of engagement for learners and members of your Academy of One.

WHY?

Reviewing the history, philosophy, and potential for evaluating performative data and social production in ways that support the learning process raises every child's favorite question:

"Why?"

Why do we evaluate learning? Is it to ensure that a person has the requisite skills to perform a complicated task, such as flying an airplane or performing surgery? Is it to identify areas for improvement? Is it to sort learners into groups and/or label them? Is it to promote compliance, raise levels of concern, intensify work habits, celebrate achievement, or convince administrators that something is actually happening in a classroom?

Rather than fighting to change policy or abolish testing, Open-Source Learning augments tests with data and metadata that can yield additional insight. Learners flourish when they are invited to decide how to demonstrate their learning and present their best work to juries of peers and mentors. They learn more effectively and they produce work of higher quality.

In school, performance is closely associated with "good" and "bad" grades. With this in mind, we must have a clear idea of what we are incentivizing and what we are discouraging. We need a clear vision.

In the next chapter, we will examine Open-Source Learning as an organizational vision that can clarify purpose and align strategy and function throughout a school.

Chapter 7

The Open-Source Learning Organization

The keenness of our vision depends not on how much we can see, but on how much we can feel.

Helen Keller[1]

Vision without execution is hallucination.

Walter Isaacson on Leonardo da Vinci[2]

The benefits of Open-Source Learning increase exponentially when the surrounding institutional system—academic department, school, or school district—supports the practice.

CASE STUDY: TRI-COUNTY EARLY COLLEGE

In 2016, Adam Haigler and Ben Owens, two teachers from North Carolina, collaborated on a grant process that led them to successfully implement Open-Source Learning throughout their school, Tri-County Early College, which is tucked away in the Blue Ridge Mountains near the borders of Tennessee and Georgia.

Haigler has an extensive background in science, outdoor education, and assessment. He described his experience with Open-Source Learning as a transformation in his thinking and his practice as a teacher:

"It's been amazing since we codified Open-Source Learning into the ground-work for our students," Haigler said. "Because the students are curating their work online, there is always a public audience. There's always a content expert from outside the school who is willing to help mentor and evaluate the students' work. It's just transformed the way we teach and learn here."

"For example, when we developed a public health project, we had 17 public health and medical professionals join our entire school for the entry event. That's how we start projects now: by bringing in the community, doing listening sessions, doing all kinds of groundwork to make sure that our kids can have authentic, relevant experiences that are strongly connected to the community."

Starting this effort was not easy.

"The year that we made all the reforms, we had tremendous institutional support. But nearing the end of the year, we had some community members and parents getting all in a huff and saying we're not teaching anymore and things like that," Haigler said. "So [the principal] sort of reigned it all in and pushed us back. That next year was a little caustic here, and a lot more concentrated power at the top. We definitely dropped into that valley of chaos and despair."

Growing pains can be intense, but they can also pay off.

"The veteran faculty stepped up and we had to have some difficult conversations," Haigler recalled. "The principal gave us back a lot of trust. She gave us back a lot of decision-making power. And now we have a $20 million-dollar Career Academy and a $200,000 grant that Ben helped negotiate, so now I have all sorts of fun digital media tools."[3]

In addition to demonstrating success through student achievement, innovative partnerships, and growth, the school is succeeding by traditional academic program metrics as well. The school has a 100 percent graduation rate, and graduates accumulate an average of 69 college credits before they leave high school.[4]

In true Open-Source Learning fashion, the process Haigler described at their school expanded to help teachers and learners elsewhere. Haigler and Owens wrote a book (*Open Up Education*, also published by Rowman & Littlefield) and they have partnered with open source software company Red Hat and a teaching institute at Duke University.

Owens, who worked for twenty years as an engineer in the private sector before teaching high school physics and math, now travels to other schools to help them develop Open-Source Learning initiatives of their own, and he sees a familiar organizational challenge on many campuses: "Working in isolation infects every school that I have collaborated with," he said. "In that environment, teachers are encouraged to compete with each other."

"Everybody says, 'Oh, I do project-based learning' when in fact they're really just doing crappy tri-folds. These teachers recognize that what we're currently doing is not serving our kids like it should. We're not preparing kids for the realities of the fourth industrial revolution. So, when I talk to them, the consistent thing is that I'm not doing window dressing on strategy. We're going to have a hard conversation that starts with your mission and vision."[5]

Yes. Let's do that.

THE BEAUTY OF THE INVISIBLE

The next two sections present the components of an effective vision, and how that differs from what most schools do with vision statements. Then we'll examine the vision of Open-Source Learning and consider ways to apply it.

First, a question: Why did those educators tell Owens that they are doing project-based learning when they are clearly not? What is he seeing that they don't?

Owens is looking deeper: "The tangible assets that learners create— tri-folds, essays, posters—are just the effects. We need to understand the causes."

This raises a simple question from the last chapter that every teacher and learner should be able to answer clearly:

Why are we doing this?

According to productivity consultant David Allen, "The *why* question . . . is nothing but advanced common sense. To know and be clear about the purpose of any activity are prime directives for appropriate focus, creative development, and cooperation."[6]

Allen should know; he has been named one of America's top five business coaches by *Forbes* and dubbed "the productivity guru" by the magazine *Fast Company*. He is best known for his book *Getting Stuff Done: The Art of Stress-Free Productivity*, which has been translated into thirty languages and used successfully by celebrities, Silicon Valley executives, and everyday people all over the world.

Instead of focusing on issues like time management or tools, or even producing work that others can see, Allen's primary focus is on clearing the mind of everything unnecessary. Without the clutter, we have the freedom to think deeply and be more creative—while getting things done.

However clear or cluttered, our state of mind is invisible. Teachers may evaluate work product, tests, online social production, and even metadata, but learners' internal efforts are easily misunderstood: one student may spend four hours on a project and produce a mediocre outcome; another student may spend eight minutes on the same project and create something brilliant.

In school, administrators often judge teachers and students by outward behaviors such as "seat time" or how busy they appear to be. Thinking deeply can look suspiciously like daydreaming or just staring off into space. Nevertheless, this is often how we do our best work. People who are successful in business, creative pursuits, sports, raising families, and other outwardly demanding endeavors swear by meditation, taking walks, and other practices that are frowned upon in traditional models of schooling.

In Open-Source Learning, students frequently create blog posts, online tools, and other artifacts that appear without an assignment from a teacher. Observers come away impressed with the students' initiative, creativity, insight, and technical skills.

Revealing the invisible is the real magic trick that Pablo pulled off back in chapter 2.

VISION

When the applause faded and his audience filed out of the classroom, still shaking their heads and uploading their "How did he do that?" posts to Instagram, I talked with Pablo about how he developed the ability to perform tasks that looked impossible.

"You know," he said slowly, "I don't think I ever really intended to perform a specific trick or even become a magician. It wasn't about achieving a goal or even finishing anything."

"What I fell in love with was the practice. I just loved figuring it out. The first time I did a trick I felt so clumsy, and I learned to expect that. From there on, I wanted to perfect the movements, just do them over and over again until there was nothing else I could possibly do to improve. I spent hour after hour on the same thing, just trying to do it better, pick it apart, get every detail right. I still do."

"In moments like this, when I connect with an audience and I hear how they respond, I feel like that is what they are really responding to—it's my practice, the way I care and want to make a good thing even better. In those moments I feel like the rest of the world sees my vision."

Pablo was onto something important. In their book *Built to Last*, Jim Collins and Jerry Porras presented a six-year study of how eighteen visionary companies set standards of excellence. These organizations' competitors were also successful, and some were also enduring, but these particular companies had a specific quality in common that made them, as Collins and Porras put it, "premiere institutions—the crown jewels—in their industries, widely admired by their peers and having a long track record of making a significant impact on the world around them."[7]

Collins and Porras found one quality that set these organizations apart. It wasn't great products (those become obsolete) or charismatic leaders (they eventually retire)—it was an understanding of abstract ideas that created an organizational culture.

Drawing on what we know about our uniquely human ability to share ideas and stories that can galvanize us to act and coordinate our activities, it makes perfect sense that the most important element of these organizational systems of belief, the one thing that has been proven to drive standards and practices to a level of unequaled excellence over time, is a made-up and invisible story: vision.

The rest of this chapter describes the components of a vision, how most school vision statements fall short, and the vision of Open-Source Learning.

RECIPE FOR A VISION

The research in *Built to Last* presents identifiable components of vision that are consistent across high-performing organizations:

- A Core Ideology
  - Core Values
  - Core Purpose
- An Envisioned Future
  - 10—30 Year BHAG (Big, Hairy, Audacious Goal)
  - Vivid Description

These ingredients inspire and drive every element of an organization, right down to the operational decisions that individuals make in the process of doing their jobs.

A sloppy vision statement can create confusion. For example, consider the organization whose vision statement says that it will be best in quality and deliver product on time every time. Sounds good, right? Now, imagine that you're an employee of that company, and you're looking at the clock three minutes before closing on a Friday afternoon. The product is almost ready to ship, but not quite. You have an impossible choice to make: *Do you get it right and send it late, or do you send it on time knowing it's not the best?*

Either way, your decision will violate the vision statement.

An organization can avoid this problem, and align everyone's efforts, by creating a vision statement that accurately describes a working philosophy that already exists. If high quality is the driving passion, forget about time. Let the quality of the work define the organization's brand and shout it from the rooftops: *We make Awesome! Sometimes that takes longer.*

A vision statement must be more than wishful thinking. It must articulate what is truly important in a way that people can reinforce with their decisions and actions.

A leader can't just write a vision statement (or a hire a consultant to do it) and then demand that others change what they've been doing all along. Everyone in the organization must understand the vision and love it (yes, *love* it) in order to effectively live it.

The vision not only clarifies the way things are done but also describes the kind of people who will be needed to continue doing things this way in the future.

SCHOOL VISION STATEMENTS

It has become popular for schools to display vision statements—and mission statements, which are frequently confused with their visionary cousins—on campus.

Search the internet using the terms "school vision statement" and you'll get thousands of results, many of which have three categories of ingredients: something about safety or caring on campus, something about personal qualities of people, and something about the future, like this: *Our vision is to educate and instill the value of safety, respect, and responsibility to ensure that our students are college and career ready.*

That vision statement is functionally worthless. "Our vision is to educate?" *Really?* You're a school! How is "educate" defined? Why is this idea important enough to be the centerpiece of the vision? How does this school's version of "educate" distinguish it from other schools? How does this vision statement define the campus experience as its lived by students and teachers every day?

Crafting a vision statement with operational integrity is no easy task. It takes time, energy, open expression, and divergent thinking.

THE OPEN-SOURCE LEARNING VISION

In most classrooms there is no awareness of a school vision statement at all. This makes articulating the organizational vision of Open-Source Learning even more important.

Students who elect to transform their classes into Open-Source Learning networks understand that they are joining a tradition with a specific vision and a history of success. They see how students in previous Open-Source Learning networks have demonstrated the principles of Open-Source Learning; these role models provide a clearer path than any syllabus.

From the beginning, co-creation is essential. Well before students get to course content, technology, or curation, they get a chance to test drive Open-Source Learning practices.

Communicating the Open-Source Learning vision does not require a formal organization where roles are defined by hierarchical authority or top-down mandates. The vision is defined and illustrated by actions that speak louder than words.

There is established precedent for this. The research literature on organizational management features models for organizational change that account for the transformative effects that occur when a group is allowed, encouraged, and empowered to imagine their own best course of action.

Consider, for example, this definition of "appreciative inquiry" created by David Cooperrider and Suresh Srivastva:

> "In its pragmatic form, 'appreciative inquiry' represents a data-based, theory-building methodology for evolving and putting into practice the collective will of a group or organization. It has one and only one aim: to provide a springboard for normative dialogue that is conducive to self-directed experimentation in social innovation."

"It must be noted, however, that the conceptual world which appreciative inquiry creates remains—despite its empirical content—an illusion," wrote Cooperrider and Srivastva. "This is important to recognize because it is precisely because of its visionary content, placed in juxtaposition to grounded examples of the extraordinary, that appreciative inquiry opens the status quo to possible transformations in collective action. It appreciates the best of 'what is' to ignite intuition of the possible and then firmly unites the two logically, caringly, and passionately into a theoretical hypothesis of an envisioned future."[8]

The belief system described here is the very same that defines our under-standing of school and so many other shared inventions. When students are first introduced to the idea of Open-Source Learning, the concept is illusory. It's a story that is so different from their lived experience that it sounds like a fantasy that is too good to be true. As students test these new beliefs, how-ever, they start to feel like they are a part of something larger. Their thinking about school and learning begins to shift, as does their performance.

Innovation does not happen in a vacuum, though, and early adopters must balance their newfound opportunity with the traditional, structural, political constraints of the larger organization in which it exists. Students in an Open-Source Learning classroom may find that their practice is different than what happens everywhere else on campus.

Therefore, understanding the larger organizational context is important. Teachers and students need to know where they can move the needle and influence the school, and where they should respect boundaries in order to preserve their corner of innovation, in case the empire strikes back. It is diffi-cult to imagine the core purpose or values of the Open-Source Learning vision conflicting with those of a larger schooling organization—but, if that happens, it would certainly be worth exploring in conversation to raise awareness and support learners.

CORE PURPOSE

Open-Source Learning champions the joy of discovery that unifies human-ity and makes the world a better place.

The missions associated with this purpose may change over time. People may develop different curriculum together, or create different types of school-ing organizations. Delivery models and teaching strategies may change.

Maybe someone will develop a platform where we can all connect and exchange learning information—maybe this will be open source, maybe it will integrate hardware. Maybe it will become the Apple, Google, or Facebook of learning.

Maybe people who read this book will start conversations that lead in entirely new, unpredictable directions (what a wonderful possibility!).

Whatever visible expressions come and go, the underlying core purpose is constant. It will forever remain the existential bedrock upon which every-thing else is built. Everything that is done under the banner of Open-Source Learning can be Owenschmarked against the core purpose, no matter how small the gesture may seem in the moment.

CORE VALUES

There are three core values of Open-Source Learning: Value, Interdependence, and Transparency.

Value

Open-Source Learning attaches tangible value to learning the moment it happens. When learners make a discovery, solve a problem, or create original work, they create value by

- Establishing a positive digital footprint that contributes to their personal brand;
- Demonstrating a capacity for attracting and energizing a community;
- Providing information and support to people who are interested in related topics;
- Contributing to the understanding and enjoyment for a wider audience;
- Raising awareness about our social systems of learning.

Case Study: Random Absence Mentoring

Lisa Malins was concerned about falling behind when she missed class. She designed a website called "Random Absence Mentoring" (randomabsence mentoring.blogspot.com) as a resource for the course. The website included a dropdown menu so that students could easily find daily journal topics, assignments, practice tests, and even a visual map of the course.

Lisa's development process illustrates how creating optimal value depends on understanding and responding to the needs of others. This is what Lloyd Tabb, founder of a business intelligence software company that was acquired for $2.6 billion, meant when he wrote, "Great software is an act of empathy. 'Whoever wrote this software had me in mind when they wrote it, and they must love me.'"[9]

Lisa's fellow students began using the site and giving Lisa feedback about additional features and content that they thought would be helpful. Lisa responded by growing the site to include two additional courses, collaborative working groups, scholarship and college finance information, and features such as a calendar, a Google group, and an interactive practice test that Lisa coded herself.

Lisa described the experience this way:

> "When I told Dr. Preston how I created the 'To Be Or Not To Be' practice test[10] on the Random Absence Mentoring website, he asked me to write a quick post about it on my blog."

"I wrote the entire thing in JavaScript, but I don't know JavaScript; I know HTML and CSS, which are nowhere near as complicated. All I did was skim through the JavaScript tutorial at the World Wide Web Consortium."

"Then I went back to the lesson with an example that looked closest to what I was trying to do, and then screwed with the code in the lesson's try-it editor until it worked. That's it."

"The moral of the story is that you don't have to know everything," Lisa wrote. "The Internet is overflowing with *free* resources, available to anyone who seeks them. If you want to create something but don't have all the technical knowledge, chances are you can find some way around it, either by learning what you don't know, finding something to copy-modify-paste, or connecting with an expert on whatever it is you need."

"Now that I think about it, I suppose that's what Open-Source Learning is all about."[11]

The value that people create through Open-Source Learning has a lasting effect. Schools like to include phrases such as "lifelong learning" in their vision statements—Open-Source Learning delivers on this promise. Five years later, Lisa posted on Twitter:

Lisa—Dr. Preston, I still think about your class from 2014. After "Laughing Heart" you asked us to memorize "To Be or Not To Be" from Hamlet, and I went off the rails and wrote a memorization test in JavaScript. That was my FIRST novel program and I'm a programmer now. Your class was special to me because you encouraged us to go off the rails, draw unlikely connections, and take those chances Bukowski mentioned.

[Reply] great to know that you're continuing what you started! What are you working on now?

Lisa—I'm a #bioinformatics intern at @MarroneBio. I'm applying my coding skills to my love of biology to help them develop effective and sustainable biopesticides. I think you'll appreciate this: to demo the bioinformatics tool #snakemake with a non-bioinformatics project, I wrote a pipeline to analyze Shakespeare characters' line counts. I call it "Snakespeare."

Interdependence

Open-Source Learning reinforces the idea that in today's globalized, specialized world, we depend on one another for nearly everything.

A research scientist for the Global Security Initiative at Arizona State University described the ways we get our needs met in today's world: "This is interdependence, which now defines us—as individuals, communities, and nations—as never before. Interdependence means that we don't all have to farm, or build houses, or make semiconductors. Instead, our complex social systems rely on the division of labor and exchange of goods and services to meet human needs. When people concentrate their labors on what each does best, all of society benefits—or so said Adam Smith in 1776 at the dawn of modern economic thinking."[12]

Interdependence runs counter to the traditional American myth of individualism. Archetypes created by Horatio Alger, Ayn Rand, and other curriculum mainstays suggest that we should somehow go it alone, transcend every obstacle, and succeed by ourselves. As Malcolm Gladwell pointed out in his book *Outliers*, "We cling to the idea that success is a simple function of individual merit and that the world in which we all grow up and the rules we choose to write as a society don't matter at all."[13]

Promoting the idea that we succeed or fail as isolated individuals who do our own work, use our own words, and keep our eyes on our own papers in a vacuum is wrong, and it does extensive damage to young people.

Human beings are social animals. We thrive in relationship with others. Developing healthy, interdependent relationships is an essential life skill.

Apart from the practicality of exchanging goods, sharing information to better understand the world, and collaborating with others to achieve what we could never achieve on our own, we have deep-seated needs to be seen, and known, and loved, and we need to see, and know, and love others. We need to depend on one another, and we need to feel that we provide value when others depend on us. We need relationships.

Our failure to address the human need for social connection has had a massive negative impact on our society. Writing in the *Harvard Business Review*, former United States Surgeon General Vivek Murthy observed, "During my years caring for patients, the most common pathology I saw was not heart disease or diabetes; it was loneliness."

"Loneliness and weak social connections are associated with a reduction in lifespan similar to that caused by smoking 15 cigarettes a day and even greater than that associated with obesity," Murthy said. "Loneliness is also associated with a greater risk of cardiovascular disease, dementia, depression, and anxiety. At work, loneliness reduces task performance, limits creativity, and impairs other aspects of executive function such as reasoning and decision-making. For our health and our work, it is imperative that we address the loneliness epidemic quickly."

"Loneliness is a growing health epidemic," said Murthy. "We live in the most technologically connected age in the history of civilization, yet rates of loneliness have doubled since the 1980s. Today, over 40 percent of adults in America report feeling lonely, and research suggests that the real number may well be higher."[14]

In Britain, so many people feel lonely that the government named a minister of loneliness. *The New York Times* quoted a statement from Prime Minister Theresa May in which she said, "For far too many people, loneliness is the sad reality of modern life. I want to confront this challenge for our society."[15]

Facilitating the type of productive working connections between students—the types of relationships that Open-Source Learning fosters—is essential to maintaining a safe, healthy social system in which everyone can learn, especially in an era when disconnection can lead to violence.

As Rhitu Chatterjee pointed out on a National Public Radio report about school shooters, "Feeling like an outcast at school may . . . play a role." Chatterjee reported the conclusions of John Van Dreal, psychologist and director of safety and risk at Salem-Keizer Public Schools: "Studies show that social rejection at school is associated with higher levels of anxiety, depression, aggression and antisocial behavior in children."[16]

Strengthening individual understanding through collaborative connection is consistent with accepted education theory. In 1930, education theorist Lev Vygotsky wrote, "As an individual only exists as a social being, as a member of some social group within whose context he follows the road of his historical development, the composition of his personality and the structure of his behavior turn out to be a quantity which is dependent on social evolution and whose main aspects are determined by the latter."

"Already in primitive societies," said Vygotsky, "which are only just taking their first steps along the road of their historical development, the entire psychological makeup of individuals can be seen to depend directly on the development of technology, the degree of development of the production forces and on the structure of that social group to which the individual belongs. Research in the field of ethnic psychology has provided incontrovertible proof that both of these factors, whose intrinsic interdependence has been established by the theory of historical materialism, are the decisive factors of the whole psychology of primitive man."[17]

When Sarah Gutierrez was a student in an Open-Source Learning network, she described how creating content and collaborating brought her closer to people:

"How are we connecting? YouTube has been a big way for me to connect with other people and people comment from all over the world. I've got people from as far away as Taiwan who are subscribed to me. They chime in sometimes and say, 'Hey, I really liked your idea on this video, it really helped me out.' So I think that sort of connection is really good."[18]

Students in Sarah's course were inspired by the early adopters, the ones who grabbed the opportunity and went on to organize a microfinance club, a hackspace, a scholarship search platform, and dozens of other projects.

Learning through connecting and collaborating with others also provides a meaningful cultural experience. Members of Open-Source Learning networks identify with each other and with a meaningful purpose. They interact with others from different backgrounds, and come to understand larger concepts of interconnectedness, including some from other cultures, such as *ubuntu*, which is usually translated as, "I am because we are."

"I want you to be all you can be," said Archbishop Desmond Tutu, "So that I can be all I can be."[19]

As Franklin Delano Roosevelt put it, "If civilization is to survive, we must cultivate the science of human relationships—the ability of all people, of all kinds to live together, in the same world at peace."[20]

Transparency

Interdependence requires trust, and trust begins with transparency—letting others see how you do what you do. Transparency can be uncomfortable, but when we get over the hurdle, it is extraordinarily liberating and rewarding.

Anyone who wants to see what's happening in a course of study should be able to click on a link and see resources, work product, and interactions.

Children are already under surveillance at school, and their images and information are all over the public internet, so the question becomes: Why do so many schools still keep things secret?

In the words of newspaper publisher Joseph Pulitzer, "There is not a crime, there is not a dodge, there is not a trick, there is not a swindle, there is not a vice which does not live by secrecy."[21]

Practicing the value of transparency is also an effective way to become a role model for courage. When students see their teacher try new things, and take calm responsibility when something goes awry, they are inspired to do likewise.

Mistakes are gold. Teachers who invite proofreading are role models in a culture where many people don't know how to ask for help. It costs nothing to admit a mistake if you're not trying to appear perfect in the first place. Students can't correct what they don't read—inviting constructive criticism increases engagement. Best of all, more eyes on the work makes it better.

On the walls of this year's classroom: mandated legal notices, an evacuation map, a fire extinguisher, and a Banksy print of a police officer spraying graffiti that says: "Blank walls are a crime." The rest of the wall is blank. There is no vision statement.

The vision is invisible. And yet, students see it. Some of them get really good at putting into practice, which creates a lot of visible experiences and artifacts. These students see it as an alternative, a possibility that challenges them to reimagine learning. It is a really nice feeling to be in a room full of people who enjoy what they're doing, especially when they enjoy helping each other and working toward constant improvement.

The vision of Open-Source Learning is intended to create a positive impact that extends beyond the classroom geographically, generationally, demographically, and into the future, as learners sustain the momentum on their own.

There are few pleasures greater in life than sampling the craft of someone who loves what they do so much that they've devoted years of their lives to get really, really good at it.

In an online conference with the MacArthur Connected Learning Alliance, Brady Redman, a former student of mine, said, "In most classes I had a huge issue with learning. I've struggled through school my entire life. Open-Source Learning is easier because there isn't one way of learning anymore."

"We each learn in our own ways with the blog and different ways to do projects," said Brady. "We get to choose how to get these things done. We get to use our minds and really get in depth with it."

"It helps everybody learn instead of just focusing on a single person because our school system itself is based on a century-old system that was made in a time when most people were illiterate. They didn't see the value of education and for years we've been stagnant."

"And now," Brady said, "in just a few class periods and one classroom, in a tiny little school district, a tiny town in this huge world, we're finally starting to move again. It makes me feel very honored and special that we're getting to open up this whole new world of education."[22]

That is quite a vision.

Chapter 8

Brick by Brick

No [one] ever wetted clay and left it, as if there would be bricks by chance and fortune.

Plutarch[1]

So far, Open-Source Learning strategies and tactics have been embedded in discussions about belief systems and theoretical frameworks that address why we do what we do.

Here are some practical next steps, framed by Frequently Asked Questions that students, teachers, parents, administrators, and community members have asked over the years.

These ideas are not presented in any particular order or sequence. Just like anything else in Open-Source Learning, you will need to decide for yourself what is important here; please feel free to adapt whatever applies to your situation, needs, and preferences.

* * *

How can I get students involved?

You can't. Students, like most people, don't like being manipulated. Stop trying to "get" them to do anything. Make the value proposition and let them decide.

Your invitation can be as simple as, "I'm wondering if there is a better way to learn together—are you willing to kick around a few ideas?"

Expect the unexpected. Maybe someone will reject your invitation, or express a need for clarification and discussion. Other ideas may emerge; be open.

Reserve ample time and energy for the conversation. The topic and the process will necessarily shift roles and renegotiate relationships. It may take longer than you expect.

Are students really able to determine what they would like to learn and share with the world?

This question takes two forms:

1) Teachers want to know if students have this ability in general; and
2) Teachers want to know if students are given that much freedom.

For (1): Yes. Students have an innate sense of curiosity and wonder about the world and their places in it. To varying degrees, students have learned to ignore their own curiosity and stop asking questions, so this ability may require some time and positive reinforcement to rehabilitate.

For (2): Yes. Apart from hurting a sentient being or breaking a law, students can choose what they want to learn and how. Freedom can't be given, it can only be taken, so students determine how far they are willing and able to take this.

Can students still study topics together, as a class, with the teacher?

Absolutely. The best way to learn is together. This can be done with Big Questions, or with traditional curriculum.

If you have not identified an area of specialization, or if this is a self-guided exploration, you might consider focusing on the things that people need to know and that school doesn't teach.

One exercise that has proven meaningful for many teachers is facilitating a Socratic seminar or unstructured discussion to ask students what they would value learning.

Consider the scope and depth of some recent ideas proposed by students:

Personal finances and taxes
Death and dying
Arduino projects
Coding
Dealing with divorce
Exercise, nutrition, and sleep
Home/car maintenance and repair
Negotiation
Cooking
Business planning
Conflict management and communication techniques, such as Restorative
    Dialogue and Non-Violent Communication

How can I lose an argument with a student and save face at the same time?

It's hard to save face when you're worried about saving face. Trust your audience. No one will think less of you for showing grace and goodwill as you learn and change your mind. Be "hard on ideas and soft on each other." Frame the argument as a collaborative search for truth, rather than a competition to be won.

Our adversarial system of law leads people to stop communicating and end relationships in pursuit of victory. But someone always loses. As a result, at least 50 percent of the parties to a lawsuit are unhappy with the result 100 percent of the time. In the classroom, there are more productive ways to navigate differences and conflicts.

Learn your way through having a good argument. Ask questions that invite thoughtful answers, listen to those answers, reflect and clarify, question the truth and validity of what you hear, and then—this is the best part—find opportunities to change your mind. Think of all the benefits: you model reciprocity, you surprise someone and maybe even make a friend, and you learn something new. This approach works equally well in-person and online, where the process requires us to organize our thoughts en route from our brain to the keyboard.

How much of Open-Source Learning involves keeping your cool?

All of it. This is less of a responsibility and more of an opportunity. Practicing Open-Source Learning makes people happier and calmer. Practice a minute of mindfulness (everyone's MOM), or take a moment to consider how ridiculous getting mad at a laser printer looks to spectators.

The less attached a teacher is to a particular perspective, the more empathetic they can be whenever someone else becomes upset, triggered, angry, or hurt. Communication is often pressurized in the fast-paced, noisy, emotionally charged environment of school. The next time your computer dies just before class, or a student says something that sets you off, try to remember that—in the grand scheme of things—it's really not that big of a deal.

Life is messy, and learning is messy, but this is part of the play, and you are on stage. The audience is watching your every move to see how you respond.

What platform(s) should I use in my work with students?

This depends on what you and your students think is the right tool for the job. Turn the students on the internet and ask them to find the tools that will answer questions such as:

- What features do you need to curate your work and tell your story online?
- Is it easy to follow, use, and navigate?

- Can you include media and features to make it friendly and engaging for users?
- Does it meet your budgetary requirements?
- Can you back up content onto your own hard drive? Can users comment?

In a fairly short period of time you will have empowered your fellow decision-makers, you will have crowdsourced applied research, and, together, you will have generated a variety of options.

Many teachers and students have a lot on their minds at the beginning of a school year, and tech research is not a welcome addition to their "to-do" list. For the basics of blogging and creating content, the most popular options are Blogger and Wordpress. Some photography students have preferred Tumblr, and others have elected to create different types of websites and used builders such as Weebly, Wix, and Duda. Or some even learn to code and create their own online platforms.

For collaboration, students can use videoconferencing tools, mind maps, collaborative documents and whiteboards, and visualization tools like word clouds.

For a list of specific platforms and tools that Open-Source Learning students have used, see page 149.

What do I need to know about the laws, rules, and etiquette regarding intellectual property on the internet?

To learn more about "netiquette," visit creativecommons.org for background about sharing academic and creative work online. Find a Creative Commons license that meets your needs and put it on your site. This will tell your viewers that (a) there is such a thing and you know about it and (b) there are specific terms and conditions under which they can copy, use, and remix your content.

The internet is a treasure trove of media that is copyright-free and royalty-free. Many well-known paintings, photographs, films, and recordings have passed into the public domain. Also, some kind-hearted creators will allow you to use their work for the asking—but do ask; don't assume. It is also important to recognize that authors, artists, composers, and other creators deserve acknowledgement and compensation for their work.

What do I need to know about online privacy and security?

Digital culture has changed drastically over the last ten years. Ironically, many schools present the internet as safer today, along with all sorts of digital tools, when the reality is that companies and bad influencers have actually refined their use of technology to make going online an increasing threat to the unsuspecting.

The Electronic Frontier Foundation (eff.org) is an excellent resource. The foundation's website includes coverage of current topics affecting the digital realm, as well as links to security tools and a resource curriculum for anyone who wants to teach digital security (which is one of the best ways to learn about it).

I see other teachers on social media; how do I put myself out there?

Start posting. You don't have to start on a public forum. You can start small and invite a select group of readers and/or students to your new blog or website.

Begin with a welcome message like this: "Hi! My name is David, and I'm excited to begin learning about (. . .). This is where I'm going to share my experiences, and I hope you'll join me! Please click the "Follow by Email" widget to get automatic updates when I post, or you can check back here every Wednesday for new material. Thanks for reading." (NOTE: In this example, you just put yourself on the hook to post at least once a week, so be prepared to keep your digital commitments.)

Reach out to friends, family, and colleagues to let them know about your project and invite them to give you feedback. When you are ready, seek out people who are accomplished in your field and do the same.

Parents and administrators want to see "rigor" and "classroom manage-ment"—what can I show them?

For rigor, take out your phone or tablet and open your internet browser. Show off the 100 percent student participation rate, and the positive comments to the course blog, and the number of page views, and the social production on student blogs.

Classroom management is never an issue in Open-Source Learning. The students learn to manage themselves. This is true at every age. Younger children can easily take responsibility for concrete tasks, and older students can assume leadership roles in their courses as they begin to understand and take responsibility for their community. Discipline, accountability, and responsibility are all considered internal qualities in Open-Source Learning.

What if I don't have departmental support or a budget?

Be self-sufficient. Do you need to do something that you don't know how to do? What a great time to learn. A wealth of free or low-cost training, background, and resources is available online. And going your own way can be a freeing experience—if you don't have to ask the institution for anything, you don't owe the institution anything.

Expect a mess. Things will break, malfunction, and take more time than you expect. Teacher credential programs and school districts paint pictures of students waiting patiently in line to take their places in assigned seats in front of organized materials and charged-up tablets, ready to learn. This sort of fiction is absurd and destructive. Creating these sorts of expectations inevitably leads to disappointment, frustration, self-doubt, and resentment.

What hardware do I need?

Any smartphone, tablet, laptop, or desktop connected to the internet will work. More than 80 percent of teenagers have smartphones and access to the internet,[2] so it is quite likely that students already have the answer to this question in their pockets.

What software, online platforms, or apps should I use?

The supply of digital tools out there is seemingly endless, and people are building new ones every day. So, rather than comb through lists of thousands, narrow the field by determining the purpose you need the tool to serve.

What do you want to create—a collaborative online document? Mind map? Word cloud? Online conference? Meme generator? There are tools for everything—examining them and comparing them is an education in itself.

In evaluating tools, consider their DNA: Were they created by a corporation, a foundation, or an individual? A tool created by a corporation will be, of course, designed to make a profit for its shareholders, and this value will in turn influence its policies and features.

As the name implies, Open-Source Learning prioritizes transparency, sharing, and collaboration. Software that requires subscription fees or security-based licenses for access are antithetical to the value of openness.

A school that requires students to use a licensed application platform such as Microsoft 365 is harvesting data at the student's expense. Functionally, the platform offers a suite of productivity services including email, word processing, spreadsheet and presentation functions, and shared notebooks. However, unless a student proactively copies or downloads all the content they create, it will all disappear when they leave the school and their account is deactivated.

Alternatives to licensed platforms exist that are free and legal to download. And most of them can be set up so documents, presentations, and data produced with them can be formatted to work seamlessly with for-profit products; for example, LibreOffice is the most popular freeware that matches up with Microsoft 365; millions worldwide use it.

If I allow students to use devices in class, won't some students use their screens for other things when they should be working?

Yes. This happens for a variety of reasons.

The opportunity here is to extend trust and reflect with each other on how that trust is honored. The classroom is a relatively safe environment in which to make mistakes. No one is going to lose a limb or their house or their family, so it is worth keeping in perspective.

Students do not have a lot of practice in exercising their independence, so they are bound to make mistakes. This is an important part of the process of growing discipline and accountability, which should come from a sense within each individual instead of being imposed and demanded by an authority figure.

If distraction forms a pattern of behavior, it may point to a cognitive or contextual issue outside the immediate learning environment. It may also point to an underlying belief system about school. Often students have already come to conclusions about school that make them resistant to everything in the classroom.

Even students who show delighted surprise at how fun and easy learning can be still fail because they do not create work product that others can see. The most common observation students make is that the process of going on the internet seems so fun that they forget it is schoolwork. As engaged as they are with the ideas, they realize they have to create and maintain routines that will help them achieve the goals they set.

Some of my students don't have a computer at home. Is it discriminatory to require students to use technology?

It is discriminatory not to. Our students are entering a world where understanding and using online tools are mandatory for success.

Some students don't have books at home, and yet we challenge them to read. Some students don't have cars, but we challenge them to get around. In public schools, right to access is most certainly an issue of equity, so here are some things you can do to ensure every student can participate:

1) Provide access to devices in the classroom as budgets and schedules allow;
2) Accept work on paper when the student cannot access a device or the internet, and teach the student how to scan and upload the image to their blog. For best images, have a scanner in the classroom and use a document site like scribd.com to convert .pdf files into HTML embed codes that can be inserted into blog posts; if that's too much, a well-lit and scaled image shot with a phone and converted to a .jpg will do the trick.

Do I need an Acceptable Use Policy?

No. What you need is common sense, humanity, and empathy. This is what people respond to. The philosophy of Open-Source Learning is to not have an Acceptable Use Policy, or a Digital Driver's License, or anything else that reeks of being a rulebook.

The use of the public internet is a chance to disprove negative stereotypes about adolescents and teenagers by showing up and proving ourselves great. No one wants to be the person who breaks the streak, dishonors the tradition, and blows it for everyone else.

This is a powerful opportunity to restore something that has been lost in our culture: the belief that most people will do the right thing most of the time.

Students in Open-Source Learning courses around the world have created millions and millions of digital artifacts. The next student who intentionally posts something inappropriate for no apparent reason will be the very first.

Chapter 9

The Horizon

The only way of discovering the limits of the possible is to venture a
little way past them into the impossible.

Arthur C. Clarke[1]

Knowledge is acquired when we succeed in fitting a new experience
into the system of concepts based on our old experience.

Understanding comes when we liberate ourselves from the old and so
make possible a direct, unmediated contact with the new, the mystery,
moment by moment, of our existence.

Aldous Huxley[2]

Our world continues to change, and our culture, our technology, our
economy, our communication, and our values change along with it. The ways
we educate ourselves and each other must also evolve.

Learning is an individual act. Learning can be infinitely nuanced. It can
change by the person, the weather, or the moment. Rather than attempting
to impose a new set of controls or standardized mandates, Open-Source
Learning proposes values and practices that can be implemented "as is" or
adapted to meet the needs of a particular learner or community.

So far, Open-Source Learning has:

- Made previously closed systems, such as school classrooms, publicly
  transparent;
- Facilitated students and teachers in co-creating learning experiences;

- Invited learners to create value, interdependence, and transparency by publicly curating their questions and interdisciplinary learning journeys online;
- Led to collaborations between people of different generations, institutions, states, and countries;
- Started a new and energized conversation about the future of education.

That last point is the next step.

The question now is: Where does the path created by Open-Source Learning lead?

* * *

Creating an Open-Source Learning environment serves as a catalyst for three important causes:

1. Open-Source Learning strengthens the case for everyone to have access to a free, open, and neutral internet;
2. Open-Source Learning promotes divergent and diverse thinking that can enrich our lives as individuals, and as members of social systems ranging from the immediate (family, workplace, community) to the global (economy, environment);
3. Open-Source Learning can help build a "Learning Economy," in which learners and people who support learning can create and trade on value.

WHO TELLS YOUR STORY?

These days, if you're not telling your own story online, you can be sure that someone else is. Someone could be using a tagged picture of you; a review of your class or business; a list of your former addresses, phone numbers, email addresses, and traffic tickets; or the metadata that shows everywhere you (or at least your phone) have been recently.

Our backgrounds and behavior have been tracked for decades; it isn't a new reality of the digital world. Our financial transactions and credit history have been aggregated and used by credit bureaus since they were known as merchant associations in the 1800s. Back then, the associations functioned much more like today's social media companies, collecting all sorts of data about personal habits—divorce, drinking, sexual orientation, physical health—as they profiled their customers.

Of course, a person is so much more than the sum of their data—a seemingly simple point. Yet every learner has a life story and a personality that is not reflected in a grade point average or a score on the SAT. And yet, systems of education and commerce settle for these simple measurements to define the futures of millions in each generation.

Open-Source Learning transforms the ability of the educational experience into the opportunity for each person to tell their own story.

What tools, platform, and media will you use to tell yours?

Open-Source Learning also gives each person a stake in gaining access to the internet, using it effectively, and preserving the internet as a public good. Access to the internet is an equity issue; your school, your library, and your community deserve to participate in the technology that is shaping our culture, our government, and our economy.

Education in the Information Age can be employed to help learners understand our relationship to digital culture and tools. And, whether we are helping frustrated parents or an ethically challenged Federal Communications Commission, we must ensure that everyone understands why unfettered access to a neutral internet is essential to compete in today's world.

FREEDOM TO CHOOSE?

Over the past few decades, advances in digital technology that make the internet accessible as a communications tool for non-programmers has created the impression that we have more power and more online opportunities than ever.

Do we?

For instance, in the marketplace for credit reporting agencies, the choices are limited. There are only four major credit reporting agencies in the United States, and consumers don't really have a choice—their financial behavior is reported to all of them. All that can individuals can do is audit their scores periodically and navigate a maze of "customer service" when there is a question or an error to be corrected.

In the business world, ongoing consolidation continues to shrink the number of large corporations—a few big engineering firms, a few big accounting firms, a few big Hollywood studios (and the number of studios seems to be shrinking by the day). The list goes on. Given how the digital landscape has grown, we are probably not going to dramatically reshape the political or economic forces that govern the internet; Amazon, Apple,

Facebook, and Google—the "Big Four" as they are sometimes called in the tech realm—are likely to continue to dominant the online world and how it evolves.

However, we *do* have choices about how to use the internet to preserve and enhance our freedom of expression, which in turn creates value and connection for each of us as individuals. Establishing that role of individual expression for the internet early in our lives is a crucial element in fostering an Open-Source Learning environment in the classroom.

THE LEARNING ECONOMY

Open-Source Learning brings learners closer to the expertise they need and respect. When students connect with leaders in fields such as technology, politics, medicine, music, art, and science, they experience so much more than any textbook could ever provide.

Teachers can teach anyone, anywhere. Open-Source Learning creates a culture of outreach. Students assume that they can invite the influential, the powerful, and the interesting to visit their classes—and they do.

Given the need for effective mentorship, support, and online skills to augment the learning experience, Open-Source Learning can open the door to a Learning Economy, a marketplace in which professionals can share their skills and learners can match their goals to more effectively meet everyone's needs.

Looking ahead, one interesting possibility is the use of the blockchain in education. Using smart contracts and distributed ledgers may enable people to see not only what learners produce but also the specific skills and knowledge they acquire, from whom, and when, in ways that allow us to verify the completeness and quality of their learning experience.

Helping both educators and learners with the values and practices of Open-Source Learning will pave the way for more sophisticated, thoughtful technological applications as well. Instead of installing more surveillance tools, for example, we can test the use of designs that support learning.

Brian Behlendorf, primary developer of the Apache Web Server and a leader in the open-source software movement, sees it this way: "Smart contracts can embed automated governance systems that can allow us to build cooperative networks and applications that are provably fair, and give us a way to do what normally we depend on institutions and regulators and inspectors and lawyers and judges to enforce. So basically you have to ask where in the education system there are agreements being made between parties. And that's . . . really about taking all of these certifications that we receive . . . and turning those into digital certificates whose integrity can be checked using blockchain technology."[3]

AN INVITATION

At the beginning of this book, "A Note to Start" made a bid for clarity and invited you to a conversation. To this point, that conversation has been rather one-sided: now it is your turn.

In reading this far, you may have found yourself:

- Reflecting on your own practice and/or saying to yourself, "Hey I've been doing this stuff for years!"
- Thinking, "Wow, maybe this would be a good time to trade worksheets for websites."
- Asking, "Who the hell does this guy think he is?"

The same forces support and hamper every trend, initiative, and movement in education. Schools districts, unions, and associations are well-organized, and they can be conduits for communication and collaboration. And, precisely because these systems are so well-organized, they can also intimidate members and chill communication and collaboration.

Collaborating with educators, students, and thought leaders all over the world has reminded me of how generous and generally delightful people can be when they are excited to share what they know.

Open-Source Learning has expanded my horizons and led me out of the classroom to teach, learn, and share all over the world: a castle in England, a cinderblock gym in Salt Lake City, a yurt in Mongolia, the top of a waterfall overlooking Yosemite Valley, an apartment in Pacoima, a New York City basement, and elsewhere. I have worked with thousands of students and teachers in trendy new school buildings and cockroach-infested trailers. I've connected with thousands more online without leaving my house. This morning I met a physician who teaches at Yale, so I could learn how to better understand medical research and predictive statistics during pandemics. Every conversation is different, and every conversation is exciting.

May the end of this book be a new beginning. The world is at least as crazy—in ways both challenging and wonderful—now as it was in chapter 1, and it is easy to worry that students are not getting what they need, and that we cannot do more—or, worse, that there is nothing left to be done because everything just seems too big and too far gone. Every thoughtful teacher asks, at one point or another: *Am I really making a difference?*

The answer is simple: Yes. You are.

Walt Whitman wrote:[4]

O Me! O life! of the questions of these recurring,
Of the endless trains of the faithless, of cities fill'd with the foolish,
Of myself forever reproaching myself, (for who more
    foolish than I, and who more faithless?)
Of eyes that vainly crave the light, of the objects mean, of the struggle ever renew'd,
Of the poor results of all, of the plodding and sordid crowds I see around me,
Of the empty and useless years of the rest, with the rest me intertwined,
The question, O me! so sad, recurring—What good amid these, O me, O life?
Answer.
That you are here—that life exists and identity,
That the powerful play goes on, and you may contribute a verse.

Please join the conversation about Open-Source Learning. Contribute your verse.

Epilogue

Happy Landings

The plane felt smaller as we flew higher. Thin panes of glass and sheets of metal seemed like nothing between me and thousands of feet of . . . nothing. It is one thing to feel awestruck and insignificant when you look at the vastness of the ocean or the night sky, but the added element of total vulnerability while in flight was a fascinating revelation; whatever I dared imagine Open-Source Learning might look like, I had not anticipated this.

I didn't have to imagine falling, because every few minutes, we did. Each time I caught my breath and managed to relax even a little bit, an updraft or air pocket threw us around the sky.

Eventually I began to enjoy the sensation. It may seem counterintuitive, but feeling tiny and powerless, like my life might end any second, was a powerful exercise in self-reflection. I had no illusion that I could control anything that was happening in or around that plane, so in that moment there was nothing to do but take it all in and enjoy the ride.

In the backseat of that plane, between the sensory experiences and observations of all the things Matt and Ed were doing, I was surprised by memories that I hadn't thought about in decades.

When I was young, before I knew anything about missed connecting flights, long security lines, and the middle seat of a rear row behind the screaming baby, I saw airplanes as symbols of adventure and possibility. My grandfather was a Lieutenant Colonel in the United States Air Force, and I grew up listening to his stories of flying military cargo planes in the Berlin Airlift and over the Himalayas ("the Hump"). My Dad was a navigator in the Air Force, and I loved it when he would drive me to the airport near our house to watch planes take off and land. My best friend Eric and I would spend hours drawing pictures of planes and imagining all the places around the world we would visit someday.

I was abruptly brought back to the present when the plane dropped—hard. The sensation shot my stomach into my throat. As I felt the sheer magic of defying gravity take me from panic to joy and back to panic again, I paused my internal slide show and concentrated on what was going on around me.

But all was calm in the front two seats. In *The Right Stuff*, author Tom Wolfe comments on the way airline pilots talk—they all seem to talk alike, and they all seem to talk like Chuck Yeager, the legendary test pilot who first flew faster than the sound barrier: cool, and collected, with a little bit of an Appalachian drawl.

Matt and Ed chatted about the microclimate—no drawls, but calm and in control, totally unaffected by our unexpected drop in altitude. Ed said, "So that's when you're tempted to make a move, but you want to read the air a little bit first," and Matt chimed in, "Yep, don't want to over correct, right?" They could have been talking while sitting together on a park bench.

We flew from Lompoc out toward Jalama Beach, then back through the Santa Maria Valley over the high school. Ed told us the story behind every landmark: "See that farm down there? That was owned by one of the first Portuguese families who emigrated here." We learned about the Native American tribes who lived in the area, agricultural practices, La Purisima Mission, and the town of Guadalupe.

Most of our learning is not so closely connected with life experiences such as Matt's. As Peter Senge suggests in his book *The Fifth Discipline*,[1] learning from direct experience can be powerful, "But what happens when we can no longer observe the consequences of our actions? What happens if the primary consequences are in the distant future or in a distant part of the larger system in which we operate?"

"We each have a 'learning horizon,' a breadth of vision in time and space within which we assess our effectiveness," Senge wrote. "When our actions have consequences beyond our learning horizon, it becomes impossible to learn from direct experience."

In school and at work, our learning horizons are further limited by the ways in which organizations tend to divide people and functions. How can teachers analyze the ways in which instruction and performance correlate and interact to create cycles over time when they work in isolation from one another on time-consuming tasks such as grading individual students? Open-Source Learning provides a structural framework and a dedicated process to help us reflect what we learn.

Doing something well is challenge enough, but replicating the success or understanding it well enough to teach someone else is impossible—unless you know exactly what made you effective in the first place. That knowledge, and the power it instills in the learner, is the essence of Open-Source Learning.

Now that he had flown a real airplane, Matt needed to learn about his experience in a structured way.

First he had to land.

As Matt descended and brought us toward the runway on final approach, I wondered how it would feel to land in a little plane. I flashed back to a flight I took from Los Angeles to Frankfurt, Germany. There was a storm. The airliner pitched and lurched uncontrollably. The last leg of the trip was so violent that most of the passengers vomited. There was a lot of crying and praying. It was like something out of a movie; I even heard a quarrelsome couple stop arguing and declare how much they loved each other. We hit the runway hard and skidded to a stop. When the doors opened, everyone cheered and headed straight for the bar.

Matt set us down softly, like a pro.

The structure and process of Open-Source Learning engages and changes everyone who participates in it. There is a Zen saying that describes the effect: "When the flower arranger arranges the flowers, he also arranges his mind and the mind of the person who looks at the flowers."

Open-Source Learning has as much to offer the instructor as it provides to the learner; we become more aware of the way we think, feel, connect the dots, look at new approaches, return to the moment, and reflect—a phenomenon I was recognizing as I realized how much those benefits were reflected in my observing how the sequence of preflight, flight, and post-flight analysis unfolded.

After we taxied to the hangar and parked the plane, Ed and Matt reviewed the flight together. Ed apparently keeps a flight recorder in his head, and I listened as he talked to Matt about his observations from the trip.

Modern tools added a dimension to their conversation. As thorough as Ed was, when he and Matt looked at the video on my phone, Ed saw a few things that he hadn't noticed in real time. Like a sportscaster breaking down a replay, Ed was able to pause the video and distill moments for Matt. Together they analyzed the factors that could influence Matt's actions in the moment. Ed explained concepts at length and described the implications of alternative decisions without the immediate concern of keeping the plane in the sky.

"You showed good instinct here," Ed said, pausing the video as Matt adjusted his course after we hit some turbulence, "just remember that you need to pick your landmarks and think ahead a little, because that's just about the time we started needing to think about fuel and the ride home."

The video and pictures also allowed Matt to share his experience with his network. This is a powerful evaluative tool.

Once upon a time, blue books and multiple-choice tests were considered the most effective ways to test what learners knew. Maybe that made sense in 1980, when one gigabyte of computer memory cost $300,000. Back then, there was no easy, affordable way to document real-time interaction or demonstrate skill mastery.

Now, we can stream and remix our learning stories in multiple mediums to share instantaneously around the world with anyone with an internet connection. It's a new day.

If you want to see how Matt Reynolds successfully took off and landed a Piper Tri-Pacer that day, check out the videos on opensourcelearning.net/flight. My video is a handheld amateur's effort; a high-resolution camera and audio recorder—these days an increasingly inexpensive tool—installed in the plane would enable Matt to document each decision and move he makes, improving his own performance and teaching others as well.

As we drove back to the high school, I thought of Matt's heroic journey: how he responded to the call of his dreams, the mentor he sought out, the forces he thought were working against him, the challenge he accepted in taking me for a flight, and his proud return to the place where he started.

None of this would have happened in the conventional classroom, in the absence of Open-Source Learning.

The vast majority of students are like Matt. They don't stand out as academic superstars. Matt wasn't a stellar student, but he also wasn't enough of a failure or a problem to warrant additional attention or support. He was quiet, bored, and less than fully functional—but only because the educational system had not been willing or able to inspire him.

Left to his own devices, Matt probably would have either done just enough to pass the course, or he would have flunked it and made up the units over the summer in the school's online credit recovery program. Maybe he would have gone to community college for a while until his transcript looked good enough to apply to the school he really wanted to attend. Or maybe not.

But given the opportunity to practice Open-Source Learning, Matt literally took off. Once Matt identified his Big Question, he pursued something that was truly important to him. Completing the course requirements became easy. He read about a subject he loved, and he wrote to express himself. The more he practiced both skills, the more he improved. With the guidance of an expert mentor, Matt was able to gain real-time experience in the world he wanted to join. He documented his learning and piloting in real time.

Clearly, Matt's experience was a unique application of Open-Source Learning. But every student has interests and dreams that are typically unfulfilled by the restrictions of the conventional classroom—restrictions that can be transformed into unique learning experiences for themselves and others—if they are shown the path.

Matt drove us back to the high school. He pulled into the parking lot and I got out of the car. Before I closed the door, I leaned back down. "Thank you," I said. "This was truly a once in a lifetime experience."

"What do you mean?" he asked.

I thought about it for a moment. "Well, for starters, it checked every Open-Source Learning box. You really dedicated yourself to doing something that required your absolute best. You created a network, you curated your learning, and along the way you managed to remind me how fortunate I am to be a part of your journey."

Matt said, "But I see you do that with a lot of students. What makes this 'once-in-a-lifetime'?"

"I am never doing this again."

Matt was still laughing as he pulled out of the driveway.

I believe that every Open-Source Learning story has a happy ending. Matt's did. He passed the course, graduated on time, and was admitted to San Jose State University, where he graduated with a BS in Aviation Operations in June 2020. Most importantly, now that he has experienced the sensation of pursuing a goal that he loves, and learned enough to feel successful, Matt is never going to settle for less.

Neither should you.

Resources for Open-Source Learning

Here are resources that Open-Source Learning teachers and students have found helpful. Although some websites charge for their services, free is always better for students. Even if you have a budget, be mindful and bring students along as you investigate—the company's "DNA" (its values/vision, its people, its creation story) is likely to show up in the software.

A never-ending stream of innovation continues online. Between the time I type this and the time you read it, developers will have created dozens of new tools and platforms. Some of those listed here may change or go away. Be on the watch, and please share what you discover and use with the Open-Source Learning community at opensourcelearning.net/contact.

By the time this book is published, many more online tools and services will be available. For the latest information, see the links below. (* Note: Inclusion here is not an endorsement.)

BLOG AND WEBSITE DEVELOPMENT

Blogs—Blogger.com, Wordpress.com, Tumblr.com
Text curation/embedding—Scribd.com
Video curation/embedding—YouTube.com, Vimeo.com

COLLABORATION

Conferencing—Skype.com, Zoom.com, Google Hangouts
Mind Maps—Mindmeister, Mindomo, Mindjet, CMAP

LINKS TO OPEN-SOURCE LEARNING MATERIAL

For general information about Open-Source Learning, including FAQs, teaching resources, and links to related sites, visit opensourcelearning.net.

All of the websites and coursework described in this book remain online for everyone to explore. A general menu to access this material is posted at opensourcelearning.net/coursework

Topic links

- The original "Big Question" post, which includes images, videos, and all students' comments: opensourcelearning.net/big-question.
- The initial blog used for some classes to introduce students to Open-Source Learning: opensourcelearning.net/will-this-blog-see-tomorrow.
- A selection of student websites and videos: opensourcelearning.net/student -blogs
- The interview by author Howard Rheingold and Open-Source Learning students: opensourcelearning.net/rheingold
- Resources on reflective listening, Non-Violent Communication, and restorative dialogue: opensourcelearning.net/collaboration
- Interviews with students, educators, and thought leaders: https:// opensourcelearning.net/perspectives
- The mindmap described in chapter 5 coauthored by 100 students in 24 hours: opensourcelearning.net/mindmap
- Sample vision statements for Open-Source Learning: opensourcelearning .net/vision

Notes

PROLOUGE

1. "Man will never fly . . ." John Noble Wilford, "Earliest Days; Takeoff! How the Wright Brothers Did What No One Else Could," *The New York Times*, December 9, 2003, https://www.nytimes.com/2003/12/09/news/earliest-days-takeof f-how-the-wright-brothers-did-what-no-one-else-could.html. Also http://www.man-willneverfly.com/.

2. "The Expository Reading and Writing Course . . ." Tony Fong, Neal Finkelstein, Rebeca Diaz, Marie Broek, and Laura Jaeger, "Evaluation of the Expository Reading and Writing Course: Findings From the Investing in Innovation Development Grant," *Wested*, accessed January 2020, https://www.wested.org/resources/evaluation-of-exp ository-reading-writing-course/.

3. "Any attempt to restore a man's inner strength . . ." Victor Frankl, *Man's Search for Meaning* (Boston, MA: Beacon Press, 1992), 84.

4. "Honestly for me high school is a waste of time . . ." Matt Reynolds, "hafta/ wanna," *Matt Reynolds Expository Comp Blog*, January 27, 2014, http://mattrey1 8exposcomp.blogspot.com/2014/01/.

5. "How did these two modest small businessmen . . ." Peter L. Jakab and Tom D. Crouch, *The Wright Brothers and the Invention of the Aerial Age* (Washington, DC: National Geographic, Smithsonian National Air and Space Museum, 2003), 15.

6. "The Wrights saw the airplane as a system . . ." Wilford, "Earliest Days; Takeoff!."

7. "I learned that courage was not the absence of fear . . ." Nelson Mandela, *Notes to the Future: Words of Wisdom* (New York, NY: Simon and Schuster, 2012), 18.

CHAPTER 1

1. Maria Vultaggio, "16 Inspirational Stephen Hawking Quotes About Life, the Universe and More," *Newsweek*, March 14, 2018, https://www.newsweek.com/steph en-hawking-quote-life-universe-aliens-dead-843692.

2. Anaïs Nin, *The Diary of Anaïs Nin*, Vol. 1, 1931–1934.

3. "We live in a world that is made of computers . . ." Cory Doctorow, "It's Not a Fax Machine Connected to a Waffle Iron," *Re:publica*, May 8, 2013, https://re-publica.com/en/session/its-not-fax-machine-connect-waffle-iron.

4. "Our goal in every education subject . . ." Laura Evenson, "Seymour Papert/ Computers in the Lives of Our Children," *SFGate*, February 2, 1997, https://www.sfg ate.com/news/article/SUNDAY-INTERVIEW-Seymour-Papert-Computers-In-2856 685.php.

5. "Standardization robs life of its spice . . ." George Sylvester Viereck, "What Life Means to Einstein," *The Saturday Evening Post*, October 26, 1929, 17, https ://www.saturdayeveningpost.com/wp-content/uploads/satevepost/what_life_means _to_einstein.pdf.

6. Wikiquote translation of *Deru kugi wa utareru.* https://en.wikiquote.org/wiki/ Japanese_proverbs.

7. "School is a place where children are compelled to be . . ." Peter Gray, "School Is A Prison – And Damaging Our Kids," *Salon*, August 26, 2013, https://www.salon .com/2013/08/26/school_is_a_prison_and_damaging_our_kids/.

8. "The traits that make successful students often stymie performance . . ." Johnny Oleksinski, "Being a Good Student Makes You A Terrible Employee," *The New York Post*, February 19, 2016, https://nypost.com/2016/02/19/being-a-good-student-makes-you-a-terrible-employee/.

9. "The fundamental issue is that law schools are . . ." David Segal, "What They Don't Teach Law School Students: Lawyering," *The New York Times*, November 19, 2011, https://www.nytimes.com/2011/11/20/business/after-law-school-associates-learn-to-be-lawyers.html.

10. "America's K-12 education system, taken as a whole, fails our nation . . ." U.S. Department of Education, *For Each and Every Child – A Strategy for Education Equity and Excellence* (Washington, DC: U.S. Department of Education, 2013), https ://www2.ed.gov/about/bdscomm/list/eec/equity-excellence-commission-report.pdf.

11. "More students are living in emergency shelters . . ." Lauren Camera, "More Students Are Homeless Than Ever Before," *U.S. News & World Report*, January 30, 2020, https://www.usnews.com/news/education-news/articles/2020-01-30/more -students-are-homeless-than-ever-before.

12. "Districts (in high poverty areas) tend to have more students in need of extra help, and yet they have fewer . . ." Alana Semuels, "Good School, Rich School: Bad School, Poor School," *The Atlantic*, August 25, 2016, https://www.theatlantic.com/bu siness/archive/2016/08/property-taxes-and-unequal-schools/497333/.

13. ". . . more than two million students . . ." U.S. Department of Education, National Center for Education Statistics, "The Condition of Education 2019," Washington, DC, 2019, *NCES 2019-144*, https://nces.ed.gov/programs/coe/indicator_coj.asp.

14. "Yet only about half of U.S. adults . . ." Stephanie Marken, "Half in U.S. Now Consider College Education Very Important," *Gallup*, December 30, 2019, https://www.gallup.com/education/272228/half-consider-college-education-important.aspx.

15. "Teachers used to base their authority . . ." Douglas Rushkoff, *Program Or Be Programmed: Ten Commands for a Digital Age* (New York, NY: OR Books, 2010), 115.

16. "79 percent of Americans said students respected teachers when . . ." Julia Ryan, "Poll: Teachers Don't Get No Respect," *The Atlantic*, January 24, 2014, https://www.theatlantic.com/education/archive/2014/01/poll-teachers-dont-get-no-respect/283318/.

17. The full text of this law can be found at https://www.mass.gov/files/document s/2016/08/ob/deludersatan.pdf.

18. "Put simply, the iPhone 6's clock is 32,600 times faster . . ." Tibi Puiu, "Your Smartphone Is Millions of Times More Powerful Than the Apollo 11 Guidance Computers," *ZME Science*, February 11, 2020, https://www.zmescience.com/science/news-science/smartphone-power-compared-to-apollo-432/.

CHAPTER 2

1. "The best works are often those . . ." Clifford Still, as quoted in *Abstract Expressionism*, ed. David Antham (London: Thames & Hudson, 1990), 137.

2. "When we are no longer able . . ." Viktor Frankl, *Man's Search for Meaning* (Boston, MA: Beacon Press, 2006). Original English-language publication in 1959 titled *From Death-Camp to Existentialism*.

3. All names of students mentioned in anecdotal content have been changed to protect their privacy.

4. "Simons and Chabris evaluated many similar studies and experiences . . ." Christopher Chabris and Dan Simons, *The Invisible Gorilla: How Our Intuitions Deceive Us* (New York, NY: Harmony, 2011), http://www.theinvisiblegorilla.com/overview.html.

5. "There are these two young fish . . ." David Foster Wallace, *This is Water: Some Thoughts, Delivered on a Significant Occasion, About Living a Compassionate Life* (New York, NY: Little, Brown & Company, 2009), https://fs.blog/2012/04/david-foster-wallace-this-is-water/.

6. "A certain ideology, along with a set of empirical assumptions . . ." Alfie Kohn, "Five Bad Education Assumptions the Media Keeps Recycling," *The Washington Post*, August 29, 2013, https://www.washingtonpost.com/news/answer-sheet/wp/2013/08/29/five-bad-education-assumptions-the-media-keeps-recycling/.

7. "The neural mechanisms for expectation processes . . ." Amanda R. Arulpragasam, Jessica A. Cooper, Makiah R. Nuutinen, and Michael T. Treadway, "Corticoinsular Circuits Encode Subjective Value Expectation and Violation for Effortful Goal-Directed Behavior," *Proceedings of the National Academy of Sciences of the United States of America (PNAS)*, January 9, 2018, https://www.pnas.org/content/115/22/E5233.

8. "Ever since the Cognitive Revolution . . ." Yuval Noah Harari, *Sapiens: A Brief History of Humankind* (New York, NY: Harper, 2015), 20–32.

9. "Americans look at their phones . . ." Lisa Eadicicco, "Americans Check Their Phones 8 Billion Times a Day," *Time Magazine*, December 15, 2015, https://time.com/4147614/smartphone-usage-us-2015/.

10. James Stafford, *Note to the Author*, May 11, 2013.

11. Ken Robinson, *Do Schools Kill Creativity?*, Filmed January 6, 2007 at TED Conference, Monterey, CA, video, 20:03, https://youtu.be/iG9CE55wbtY.

12. "Public schools were not only created in the interests of industrialism . . ." Ken Robinson, *The Element: How Finding Your Passion Changes Everything* (New York, NY: Penguin, 2009).

13. "According to the latest Gallup . . ." Justin McCarthy, "U.S. Confidence in Organized Religion Remains Low," *Gallup*, July 8, 2019, https://news.gallup.com/poll/259964/confidence-organized-religion-remains-low.aspx.

14. "The existence of dissonance, being psychologically uncomfortable . . ." Leon Festinger, *A Theory of Cognitive Dissonance* (Palo Alto, CA: Stanford University Press, 1957), 3, https://books.google.com/books/about/A_Theory_of_Cognitive_Dissonance.html?id=voeQ-8CASacC.

15. "We oppose the teaching of . . . critical thinking skills . . ." Valerie Strauss, "Texas GOP Rejects 'Critical Thinking' Skills. Really," *The Washington Post*, July 9, 2012, https://www.washingtonpost.com/blogs/answer-sheet/post/texas-gop-rejects-critical-thinking-skills-really/2012/07/08/gJQAHNpFXW_blog.html.

16. Marcus Aurelius, *Meditations* (c. 121–180 AD), Vol. 20, Hays translation.

17. "A blunder—apparently the merest chance—reveals an unsuspected world . . ." Joseph Campbell, *The Hero With a Thousand Faces* (Princeton, NJ: Princeton University Press, 1949), 51.

18. "Historical experience suggests that the principal mechanism for convergence . . ." Thomas Piketty, *Capital in the Twenty-First Century* (Cambridge, MA: The Belknap Press of Harvard University Press, 2014), 22.

19. "According to the National Center for Education Statistics . . ." U.S. Department of Education, National Center for Education Statistics, *Digest of Education Statistics: 2018* (Washington, DC, 2019), https://nces.ed.gov/programs/digest/d18/.

20. "Student loan debt in America has grown . . ." Zack Friedman, "Student Loan Debt Statistics in 2020: A Record $1.6 Trillion," *Forbes Magazine*, February 3, 2020, https://www.forbes.com/sites/zackfriedman/2020/02/03/student-loan-debt-statistics/#2ef9d83281fe.

21. "The gap between the richest and the poorest households in America . . ." Bill Chappell, "U.S. Income Inequality Worsens, Widening to a New Gap," *National Public Radio*, https://www.npr.org/2019/09/26/764654623/u-s-income-inequality-worsens-widening-to-a-new-gap.

22. "I propose to call the rites . . ." Arthur van Gannep, *The Rites of Passage* (London: Routledge, 1960, reprinted 2004), 21, https://books.google.co.uk/books/about/The_Rites_of_Passage.html?id=kJpkBH7mB7oC.

23. "During the intervening 'liminal' period . . ." Victor Turner, "Betwixt and Between: The Liminal Period in Rites de Passage," in *The Forest of Symbols: Aspects of Ndembu Ritual* (Ithaca, NY: Cornell University Press, 1967), 94.

24. "As with almost all teaching positions in the United States . . ." David Graeber, *Bullshit Jobs: A Theory* (New York, NY: Simon & Schuster, 2018), 79.

CHAPTER 3

1. Buckminster Fuller, *Operating Manual for Spaceship Earth*, 1963, Chapter 6, accessed at Buckminster Fuller Institute, https://web.archive.org/web/201008231215 37/ http://www.bfi.org/about-bucky/resources/books/operating-manual-spaceship-e arth/chapter-6-synergy.

2. Vince Cruz, "608," *Vincent Cruz's AP Lit Comp Blog*, February 11, 2014, http://vcruzrhsenglitcom.blogspot.com/2013/05/608.html.

3. "The apple may not have hit Newton . . ." Amanda Gefter, "Newton's Apple: The Real Story," *NewScientist*, January 18, 2010, https://www.newscientist.com/article/2170052-newtons-apple-the-real-story/.

4. "Archimedes may not have run naked . . ." David Biello, "Fact or Fiction?: Archimedes Coined the Term 'Eureka!' in the Bath," *Scientific American*, December 8, 2006, https://www.scientificamerican.com/article/fact-or-fiction-archimede/.

5. "Researchers who study the human brain . . ." Harry Haroutioun Haladjian, "Informavores: Beings That Produce and Consume Information," *Psychology Today*, March 28, 2109, https://www.psychologytoday.com/intl/blog/theory-consciousness/201903/informavores-beings-produce-and-consume-information.

6. N. S. Gill, "Epicurus and His Philosophy of Pleasure," *ThoughtCo*, February 11, 2020, https://www.thoughtco.com/epicurus-and-his-philosophy-of-pleasure-120295.

7. "If you hear a voice within you . . ." Steven Naifeh and Gregory White Smith, *Van Gogh: The Life* (New York, NY: Random House, 2011), 362.

8. "Students learn math best when they . . ." Clifton B. Parker, "Research Shows the Best Ways to Learn Math," *Stanford Graduate School of Education*, January 29, 2015, https://ed.stanford.edu/news/learning-math-without-fear.

9. "A mood of cumulative futility . . ." Jonathan Kozol, *Savage Inequalities* (New York, NY: Harper Perennial, 1992), 137.

10. "Were it not for the pay, the time away from . . ." Nínive Clements Calegari, Daniel Moulthrop, and Dave Eggers, *Teachers Have It Easy: The Big Sacrifices and Small Salaries of America's Teachers* (New York, NY: The New Press, 2005), 22.

11. "Design is a social instrument . . ." Sarah Williams Goldhagen, *Welcome to Your World: How the Built Environment Shapes Our Lives* (New York, NY: HarperCollins, 2017), 218.

12. My previous classroom did have a graffiti wall. It was so convincing that police officers saw it as they walked by, entered the classroom with their hands on their guns, and loudly asked if everything was okay. One of the officers started reading the graffiti, got to a quote by Hunter S. Thompson, and then he read the "History of Graffiti" sign on construction paper. The officer laughed out loud and said, "Oh, man, we thought we were looking at a crime scene."

13. Cruz, "608."

14. "Mindfulness training improved both . . ." Michael D. Mrazek, Michael S. Franklin, Dawa Tarchin Phillips, Benjamin Baird, and Jonathan W. Schooler, "Mindfulness Training Improves Working Memory Capacity and GRE Performance While Reducing Mind Wandering," *Association of Psychological Science*, March 28, 2013, https://journals.sagepub.com/doi/10.1177/0956797612459659.

15. "Pavlov's research originally had little to do with psychology . . ." Michael Specter, "Drool: Ivan Pavlov's Real Quest," *The New Yorker*, November 17, 2014, https://www.newyorker.com/magazine/2014/11/24/drool.

16. "As with all of our other institutions . . ." Ray Kurzweil, *The Singularity is Near* (New York, NY: Penguin Books, 2006), 336–37.

17. "A future period during which the pace . . ." Kurzweil, *The Singularity is Near*, 7.

18. "If we just ask different questions about a problem . . ." Frans Johansson, *The Medici Effect: What Elephants and Epidemics Can Teach Us About Innovation* (Boston, MA: Harvard Business School Press, 2006), 58.

19. "These translators may see the beat of healthy . . ." Edwards, *Artscience*, 71.

20. "This is the true Galilean revolution . . ." Ivar Ekeland, *The Best of All Possible Worlds: Mathematics and Destiny* (Chicago, IL: University of Chicago Press, 2006), 9.

21. "We ask about 100 questions a day as preschoolers . . ." Po Bronson and Ashley Merryman, "The Creativity Crisis," *Newsweek*, July 10, 2010, https://www.newsweek.com/creativity-crisis-74665.

22. "Metaphor is not just a matter of language . . ." George Lakoff and Mark Johnson, *Metaphors We Live By* (Chicago, IL: University of Chicago Press, 2003), 6.

23. We are ranked, categorized, and scored . . ." Cathy O'Neil, *Weapons of Math Destruction: How Big Data Increases Inequality and Threatens Democracy* (New York, NY: Broadway Books, 2016), 70.

24. "No 'ism or 'ology has ever . . ." W. Grant Hague, *The Eugenic Marriage: A Personal Guide to the New Science of Better Living and Better Babies*, Vol. I of IV (New York, NY: The Review of Reviews Company, 1914), 651, https://www.gutenberg.org/files/21418/21418-h/21418-h.htm.

CHAPTER 4

1. "It's an open question . . ." David Preston, "Will This Blog See Tomorrow?," *Dr. Preston's English Literature & Composition 2014–2015*, May 28, 2014, https://drprestonsrhsenglitcomp14.blogspot.com/2014/05/will-this-blog-see-tomorrow.html.

2. "One reason that written testaments are effective . . ." Robert Cialdini, *Influence: The Psychology of Persuasion* (New York, NY: Harper, 2007), 81.

3. "Dignifying errors to promote learning . . ." Madeline Hunter, *Mastery Teaching: Increasing Instructional Effectiveness in Elementary, Secondary Schools, Colleges and Universities* (El Segundo, CA: TIP Publications, 1991), 87–90.

4. "Many teachers are excellent individual listeners . . ." Experienced educators and mediators may recognize some of the techniques here as reflective listening, Non-Violent Communication, and restorative dialogue. You can read more about these in the Resources section on page 150.

5. "Does your right to your opinion oblige me . . ." Jamie Whyte, *Crimes Against Logic: Exposing the Bogus Arguments of Politicians, Priests, Journalists, and Other Serial Offenders* (New York, NY: McGraw-Hill, 2005), 8.

CHAPTER 5

1. Cited in *Al Gore's Nobel Lecture*, Oslo, December 10, 2007, Transcript accessed at https://www.nobelprize.org/prizes/peace/2007/gore/26118-al-gore-nobel-lecture-2007/.
2. "I shared an interview with science-fiction author William Gibson . . ." David Wallace-Wells, "William Gibson, The Art of Fiction No. 211," *The Paris Review*, Issue 197, Summer 2011, https://www.theparisreview.org/interviews/6089/the-art-of -fiction-no-211-william-gibson.
3. "Smart mobs consist of people who . . ." Howard Rheingold, *Smart Mobs: The Next Social Revolution* (Cambridge, MA: Perseus, 2002), xii.
4. "We will have a maximum of 24 hours to complete . . ." David Preston, "Brain With 200 Legs," *Dr. Preston's Literature & Composition*, December 4, 2011, https:/ /drprestonsrhsenglitcomp.blogspot.com/2011/12/brain-with-200-legs.html.
5. "Should we all start in the same section . . ." David Preston, "December 8," *Dr. Preston's Literature & Composition*, December 8, 2011, https://drprestonsrhsengl itcomp.blogspot.com/2011/12/december-8.html.
6. Tom Gruber, *Conversation with the Author*, July 7, 2012.
7. "The basic tool for the manipulation of reality . . ." Philip K. Dick, "How To Build a Universe That Doesn't Fall Apart Two Days Later," in *The Shifting Realities of Philip K. Dick: Selected Literary and Philosophical Writings* (New York, NY: Vintage Books, 1996), 265.
8. "To me there's nothing like creation . . ." Terry Lawless in class discussion, *Dr. Preston's English Literature & Composition 2013–2014*, March 11, 2014, https:// drprestonsrhsenglitcomp13.blogspot.com/2014/03/notes-from-terry-lawless.html.
9. "The scope of action allowed to the students . . ." Paolo Freire, *Pedagogy of the Oppressed* (New York, NY: Continuum, 1993), 53.

CHAPTER 6

1. Louis D. Brandeis, "An Address Delivered before the New England Dry Goods Association at Boston, February 11, 1908," published in *Business: A Profession*, 1914, Chapter 16, accessed March 2020 at https://louisville.edu/law/library/special -collections/the-louis-d.-brandeis-collection/business-a-profession-chapter-16.
2. "Politicians use statistics . . ." Andrew Lang (1910 speech), in *Chambers Dictionary of Quotations*, eds. Don Currie and Una McGovern (London: Chambers Harrap, 2005), 488.
3. "Instead of viewing shame as a powerful . . ." James Twitchell, *For Shame: The Loss of Common Decency in American Culture* (New York, NY: St. Martin's Griffin, 1997), 15.

4. "The Houston Astros were caught cheating ..." Stephanie Apstein, "Astros Fumble Yet Another Apology for Cheating," *Sports Illustrated*, February 13, 2020, https://www.si.com/mlb/2020/02/13/houston-astros-apology-sign-stealing.

5. For an overview of Binet's Work, visit https://en.wikipedia.org/wiki/Stanford %E2%80%93Binet_Intelligence_Scales#Development.

6. Lewis M. Terman, *The Measurement of Intelligence* (Cambridge, MA: The Riverside Press, 1916), available at http://www.gutenberg.org/ebooks/20662.

7. An overview of Yerkes' Army testing can be found at https://en.wikipedia.org /wiki/Army_Alpha.

8. "The major impact of the tests . . ." Stephen Jay Gould, *The Mismeasure of Man* (New York, NY: W. W. Norton & Company, 1996), 225.

9. "Multiple choice data is garbage . . ." James E. Bruno, *Conversation with the Author*, March 9, 1995.

10. To learn more about sabermetrics, go to *A Guide to Sabermetric Research* at https://sabr.org/sabermetrics.

11. "Here we have a basketball mystery . . ." Michael Lewis, "The No-Stats All-Star," *New York Times Magazine*, February 13, 2009, accessed at https://www. nytimes.com/2009/02/15/magazine/15Battier-t.html.

12. https://www.usability.gov/.

CHAPTER 7

1. "The keenness of our vision . . ." Helen Keller, *The World I Live In and Optimism: A Collection of Essays* (Mineola, NY: Dover, 2010), 41.

2. Walter Isaacson, *Leonardo da Vinci* (New York, NY: Simon & Schuster, 2017), 4.

3. "It's been amazing since we codified Open-Source Learning . . ." Adam Haigler, *Conversation with the Author*, February 4, 2020.

4. https://www.tricountyearlycollege.org/.

5. "Working in isolation infects every school . . ." Owens Owens, *Conversation with the Author*, February 4, 2020.

6. "It never hurts to ask the why question . . ." David Allen, *Getting Things Done: The Art of Stress-Free Productivity* (New York, NY: Penguin Books, 2015), 65.

7. "Premiere institutions—the crown jewels—in their industries . . ." James Collins and Jerry Porras, *Built to Last* (New York, NY: HarperBusiness, 1997), 1.

8. "In its pragmatic form appreciative inquiry represents . . ." David Cooperrider and Suresh Srivastva, "Appreciative Inquiry in Organizational Life," in *Research in Organizational Change and Development*, Vol. 1, eds. R. W. Woodman and W. A. Pasmore (Stamford, CT: JAI Press, 1987), 129–69.

9. "Great software is an act of empathy . . ." Lloyd Tabb, "Great Software Is an Act of Empathy," *lloydtabb*, August 19, 2013, http://lloydtabb.com/great-software-is -an-act-of-empathy.

10. The "To Be or Not to Be" practice test can be found at http://randomabsence mentoring.blogspot.com/p/hamlet-practice-test.html.

11. "When I told Dr. Preston how I created . . ." Lisa Malins, "Adventures in Computer Code," *Lisa Malins AP Lit Blog*, October 22, 2013, https://lisamalinsaplit.blogspot.com/2013/10/adventures-in-computer-code.html.

12. "This is interdependence, which now defines us . . ." Shade Shutters, "Human Society is Totally Interdependent–That's a Huge Advantage, But Also a Huge Survival Risk," *Quartz*, May 2, 2017, https://qz.com/960232/human-society-is-totally-interdependent-thats-a-huge-advantage-but-also-a-huge-survival-risk/.

13. "We cling to the idea that success . . ." Malcolm Gladwell, *Outliers* (New York, NY: Little, Brown and Company, 2008), 33.

14. "During my years caring for patients, the most common pathology I saw . . ." Vivek Murthy, "Work and the Loneliness Epidemic," *Harvard Business Review*, September, 2017, https://hbr.org/cover-story/2017/09/work-and-the-loneliness-epidemic.

15. "For far too many people, loneliness is the sad reality . . ." Ceylan Yeginsu, "U.K. Appoints a Minister for Loneliness," *The New York Times*, https://www.nytimes.com/2018/01/17/world/europe/uk-britain-loneliness.html.

16. Rhitu Chatterjee, "School Shooters: What's Their Path to Violence?" *All Things Considered, National Public Radio*, February 10, 2019, https://www.npr.org/sections/health-shots/2019/02/10/690372199/school-shooters-whats-their-path-to-violence.

17. "As an individual only exists as a social being . . ." Lev Vygotsky, "The Socialist Alteration of Man," (first published 1930), in *Vygotsky Reader*, eds. René van der Veer and Jaan Valsiner (Oxford, UK: Blackwell, 1994), https://www.marxists.org/archive/vygotsky/works/1930/socialism.htm.

18. "How are we connecting? ..." Sarah Gutierrez, "This Ain't Your Grandma's School: The Transformative Power of Open-Source Learning," *MacArthur Foundation Connected Learning Alliance*, 59:20, https://youtu.be/WYnF8RT04U4.

19. Archbishop Desmond Tutu, *Ubuntu Discussion with Students during Semester at Sea 2007*, Posted March 3, 2013 by the Desmond Tutu Peace Foundation, https://www.youtube.com/watch?v=gWZHx9DJR-M, 00:52.

20. Franklin D. Roosevelt, "Franklin D. Roosevelt's Last Message to the American People," *Library of Congress Archives*, April 12, 1945, https://www.loc.gov/resource/rbpe.24204300/?st=text.

21. "In the words of newspaper publisher Joseph Pulitzer . . ." Denis Brian, *Pulitzer: A Life* (New York, NY: John Wiley and Sons, 2001), 377.

22. "In an online conference . . ." Brady Redman, "This Ain't Your Grandma's School: The Transformative Power of Open-Source Learning," *Online Conference with the MacArthur Foundation Connected Learning Alliance*, October 25, 2012, 52:09, https://youtu.be/WYnF8RT04U4.

CHAPTER 8

1. "No [one] ever wetted clay . . ." Plutarch, *Essays and Miscellanies* (New York, NY: Little, Brown, 1905), 499, https://www.gutenberg.org/files/3052/3052-h/3052-h.htm.

2. "More than 80 percent of teenagers . . ." Anya Kamenetz, "It's A Smartphone Life: More Than Half of U.S. Children Now Have One," *National Public Radio: Education*, October 31, 2019, 12:05 PM ET.

CHAPTER 9

1. Arthur C. Clark, "Hazards of Prophecy: The Failure of Imagination," in *Profiles of the Future* (New York, NY: Henry Holt & Co, 1962).

2. Aldous Huxley, *Tomorrow and Tomorrow and Tomorrow and Other Essays* (New York, NY: Harper & Brothers, 1952), 33.

3. "Smart contracts can embed automated . . ." Brian Behlendorf, *Phone Conversation with Author*, December 11, 2019.

4. Walt Whitman, *Leaves of Grass* (Mount Vernon, NY: Peter Pauper Press, 1891).

EPILOGUE

1. Peter M. Senge, *The Fifth Discipline: The Art and Practice of the Learning Organization* (New York, NY: Currency/Doubleday, 1990), 23.

Bibliography

Allen, David. *Getting Things Done: The Art of Stress-Free Productivity*. New York, NY: Penguin Books, 2015.

Apstein, Stephanie. "Astros Fumble Yet Another Apology for Cheating." *Sports Illustrated*, February 13, 2020. https://www.si.com/mlb/2020/02/13/houston-astros -apology-sign-stealing.

Arulpragasam, Amanda R., Jessica A. Cooper, Makiah R. Nuutinen, and Michael T. Treadway, "Corticoinsular Circuits Encode Subjective Value Expectation and Violation for Effortful Goal-Directed Behavior." In *Proceedings of the National Academy of Sciences of the United States of America (PNAS)*, January 9, 2018. https://www.pnas.org/content/115/22/E5233.

Aurelius, Marcus. *Meditations*. New York, NY: Modern Library, 2002.

Behlendorf, Brian. *Phone Conversation with Author*, December 11, 2019.

Biello, David. "Fact or Fiction?: Archimedes Coined the Term "Eureka!" in the Bath." *Scientific American*, December 8, 2006. https://www.scientificamerican .com/article/fact-or-fiction-archimede/.

Brian, Denis. *Pulitzer: A Life*. New York, NY: John Wiley and Sons, 2001.

Bronson, Po and Ashley Merryman. "The Creativity Crisis." *Newsweek*, July 10, 2010. https://www.newsweek.com/creativity-crisis-74665.

Calegari, Nínive Clements, Daniel Moulthrop, and Dave Eggers. *Teachers Have It Easy: The Big Sacrifices and Small Salaries of America's Teachers*. New York, NY: The New Press, 2005.

Camera, Lauren. "More Students Are Homeless Than Ever Before." *U.S. News & World Report*, January 30, 2020. https://www.usnews.com/news/education-news/ articles/2020-01-30/more-students-are-homeless-than-ever-before.

Campbell, Joseph. *The Hero With a Thousand Faces*. Princeton, NJ: Princeton University Press, 1949.

Chabris, Christopher and Dan Simons. *The Invisible Gorilla: How Our Intuitions Deceive Us*. New York, NY: Harmony, 2011.

Chappell, Bill. "U.S. Income Inequality Worsens, Widening to a New Gap." *National Public Radio*, September 26, 2019. https://www.npr.org/2019/09/26/764654623/u-s-income-inequality-worsens-widening-to-a-new-gap.

Chatterjee, Rhitu. "School Shooters: What's Their Path to Violence?" *All Things Considered, National Public Radio*, February 10, 2019. https://www.npr.org/sections/health-shots/2019/02/10/690372199/school-shooters-whats-their-path-to-violence.

Cialdini, Robert. *Influence: The Psychology of Persuasion*. New York, NY: Harper, 2007.

Collins, James and Jerry Porras. *Built to Last*. New York, NY: HarperBusiness, 1997.

Cooperrider, David and Suresh Srivastva. "Appreciative Inquiry in Organizational Life." In *Research in Organizational Change and Development*, Vol. 1, edited by R. W. Woodman and W. A. Pasmore, 129–169. Stamford, CT: JAI Press, 1987.

Cruz, Vincent. "608." *Vincent Cruz's AP Lit Comp Blog*, February 11, 2014. http://vcruzrhsenglitcom.blogspot.com/2013/05/608.html.

Dick, Philip K. *The Shifting Realities of Philip K. Dick: Selected Literary and Philosophical Writings*. New York, NY: Vintage Books, 1996.

Doctorow, Cory. "It's Not a Fax Machine Connected to a Waffle Iron." *Re:publica*, May 8, 2013. https://re-publica.com/en/session/its-not-fax-machine-connect-waffle-iron.

Eadicicco, Lisa. "Americans Check Their Phones 8 Billion Times a Day." *Time Magazine*, December 15, 2015. https://time.com/4147614/smartphone-usage-us-2015/.

Edwards, David. *Artscience: Creativity in the Post-Google Generation*. Cambridge, MA: Harvard University Press, 2008.

Ekeland, Ivar. *The Best of All Possible Worlds: Mathematics and Destiny*. Chicago, IL: University of Chicago Press, 2006.

Evenson, Laura. "Seymour Papert/ Computers in the Lives of Our Children." *SFGate*, February 2, 1997. https://www.sfgate.com/news/article/SUNDAY-INTERVIEW-Seymour-Papert-Computers-In-2856685.php.

Festinger, Leon. *A Theory of Cognitive Dissonance*. Palo Alto, CA: Stanford University Press, 1957.

Fong, Tony, Neal Finkelstein, Rebeca Diaz, Marie Broek, and Laura Jaeger. "Evaluation of the Expository Reading and Writing Course: Findings From the Investing in Innovation Development Grant." *Wested*, accessed January 2020. https://www.wested.org/resources/evaluation-of-expository-reading-writing-course/.

Frankl, Victor. *Man's Search for Meaning*. Boston, MA: Beacon Press, 1992.

Friedman, Zack. "Student Loan Debt Statistics in 2020: A Record $1.6 Trillion." *Forbes Magazine*, February 3, 2020. https://www.forbes.com/sites/zackfriedman/2020/02/03/student-loan-debt-statistics/#2ef9d83281fe.

Freire, Paolo. *Pedagogy of the Oppressed*. New York, NY: Continuum, 1993.

Gefter, Amanda. "Newton's Apple: The Real Story." *NewScientist*, January 18, 2010. https://www.newscientist.com/article/2170052-newtons-apple-the-real-story/.

Gill, N. S. "Epicurus and His Philosophy of Pleasure." *ThoughtCo*, February 11, 2020. https://www.thoughtco.com/epicurus-and-his-philosophy-of-pleasure-120295.

Gladwell, Malcolm. *Outliers*. New York, NY: Little, Brown and Company, 2008.

Goldhagen, Sarah Williams. *Welcome to Your World: How the Built Environment Shapes Our Lives*. New York, NY: HarperCollins, 2017.

Gould, Stephen Jay. *The Mismeasure of Man*. New York, NY: W. W. Norton & Company, 1996.

Graeber, David. *Bullshit Jobs: A Theory*. New York, NY: Simon & Schuster, 2018.

Gray, Peter. "School Is A Prison – And Damaging Our Kids." *Salon*, August 26, 2013. https://www.salon.com/2013/08/26/school_is_a_prison_and_damaging_our _kids/.

Gutierrez, Sarah. "This Ain't Your Grandma's School: The Transformative Power of Open-Source Learning." *MacArthur Foundation Connected Learning Alliance*, 59:20. https://youtu.be/WYnF8RT04U4.

Hague, W. Grant. *The Eugenic Marriage: A Personal Guide to the New Science of Better Living and Better Babies*, Vol. I of IV. New York, NY: The Review of Reviews Company, 1914. https://www.gutenberg.org/files/21418/21418-h/21418 -h.htm.

Haladjian, Harry Haroutioun. "Informavores: Beings That Produce and Consume Information." *Psychology Today*, March 28, 2019. https://www.psychology today.com/intl/blog/theory-consciousness/201903/informavores-beings-produce- and-consume-information.

Harari, Yuval Noah. *Sapiens: A Brief History of Humankind*. New York, NY: Harper, 2015.

Hunter, Madeline. *Mastery Teaching: Increasing Instructional Effectiveness in Elementary, Secondary Schools, Colleges and Universities*. El Segundo, CA: TIP Publications, 1991.

Jakab, Peter L. and Tom D. Crouch. *The Wright Brothers and the Invention of the Aerial Age*. Washington, DC: National Geographic, Smithsonian National Air and Space Museum, 2003.

Johansson, Frans. *The Medici Effect: What Elephants and Epidemics Can Teach Us about Innovation*. Boston, MA: Harvard Business School Press, 2006.

Kamenetz, Anya. "It's A Smartphone Life: More Than Half of U.S. Children Now Have One." *National Public Radio: Education*, October 31, 2019. https://www.npr .org/2019/10/31/774838891/its-a-smartphone-life-more-than-half-of-u-s-children -now-have-one.

Kohn, Alfie. "Five Bad Education Assumptions the Media Keeps Recycling." *The Washington Post*, August 29, 2013. https://www.washingtonpost.com/news/ answer-sheet/wp/2013/08/29/five-bad-education-assumptions-the-media-keeps- recycling/.

Kozol, Jonathan Kozol. *Savage Inequalities*. New York, NY: Harper Perennial, 1992.

Kurzweil, Ray. *The Singularity is Near*. New York, NY: Penguin Books, 2006.

Lakoff, George and Mark Johnson. *Metaphors We Live By*. Chicago, IL: University of Chicago Press, 2003.

Lawless, Terry. "Notes From Terry Lawless." *Dr. Preston's English Literature & Composition 2013–2014*, March 11, 2014. https://drprestonsrhsenglitcomp13. blogspot.com/2014/03/notes-from-terry-lawless.html.

Lewis, Michael. "The No-Stats All-Star." *The New York Times Magazine*, February 13, 2009. https://www.nytimes.com/2009/02/15/magazine/15Battier-t.html.

Malins, Lisa. "Adventures in Computer Code." *Lisa Malins AP Lit Blog*, October 22, 2013. https://lisamalinsaplit.blogspot.com/2013/10/adventures-in-computer-code.html.

Mandela, Nelson. *Notes to the Future: Words of Wisdom*. New York, NY: Simon and Schuster, 2012.

Marken, Stephanie. "Half in U.S. Now Consider College Education Very Important." *Gallup*, December 30, 2019. https://www.gallup.com/education/272228/half-consider-college-education-important.aspx.

McCarthy, Justin. "U.S. Confidence in Organized Religion Remains Low." *Gallup*, July 8, 2019. https://news.gallup.com/poll/259964/confidence-organized-religion-remains-low.aspx.

Mrazek, Michael D., Michael S. Franklin, Dawa Tarchin Phillips, Benjamin Baird, and Jonathan W. Schooler. "Mindfulness Training Improves Working Memory Capacity and GRE Performance While Reducing Mind Wandering." *Association of Psychological Science*, March 28, 2013. https://journals.sagepub.com/doi/10.1177/0956797612459659.

Murthy, Vivek. "Work and the Loneliness Epidemic." *Harvard Business Review*, September, 2017. https://hbr.org/cover-story/2017/09/work-and-the-loneliness-epidemic.

Naifeh, Steven and Gregory White Smith. *Van Gogh: The Life*. New York, NY: Random House, 2011.

Oleksinski, Johnny. "Being a Good Student Makes You A Terrible Employee." *The New York Post*, February 19, 2016. https://nypost.com/2016/02/19/being-a-good-student-makes-you-a-terrible-employee/.

O'Neil, Cathy. *Weapons of Math Destruction: How Big Data Increases Inequality and Threatens Democracy*. New York, NY: Broadway Books, 2016.

Parker, Clifton B. "Research Shows the Best Ways to Learn Math." *Stanford Graduate School of Education*, January 29, 2015. https://ed.stanford.edu/news/learning-math-without-fear.

Piketty, Thomas. *Capital in the Twenty-First Century*. Cambridge, MA: The Belknap Press of Harvard University Press, 2014.

Preston, David. "Brain With 200 Legs." *Dr. Preston's Literature & Composition*, December 4, 2011. https://drprestonsrhsenglitcomp.blogspot.com/2011/12/brain-with-200-legs.html.

Preston, David. "December 8." *Dr. Preston's Literature & Composition*, December 8, 2011. https://drprestonsrhsenglitcomp.blogspot.com/2011/12/december-8.html.

Preston, David. "Will This Blog See Tomorrow?" *Dr. Preston's English Literature & Composition 2014–2015*, May 28, 2014. https://drprestonsrhsenglitcomp14.blogspot.com/2014/05/will-this-blog-see-tomorrow.html.

Puiu, Tibi. "Your Smartphone Is Millions of Times More Powerful Than the Apollo 11 Guidance Computers." *ZME Science*, February 11, 2020. https://www.zmescience.com/science/news-science/smartphone-power-compared-to-apollo-432/.

Redman, Brady. "This Ain't Your Grandma's School: The Transformative Power of Open-Source Learning." *Online Conference with the MacArthur Foundation Connected Learning Alliance*, October 25, 2012, 52:09. https://youtu.be/ WYnF8RT04U4.

Reynolds, Matt. "hafta/wanna." *Matt Reynolds Expository Comp Blog*, January 27, 2014. http://mattrey18exposcomp.blogspot.com/2014/01/.

Rheingold, Howard. *Smart Mobs: The Next Social Revolution*. Cambridge, MA: Perseus, 2002.

Robinson, Ken. *The Element: How Finding Your Passion Changes Everything*. New York, NY: Penguin, 2009.

Roosevelt, Franklin D. "Franklin D. Roosevelt's Last Message to the American People." *Library of Congress Archives*, April 12, 1945. https://www.loc.gov/resource/ rbpe.24204300/?st=text.

Rushkoff, Douglas. *Program Or Be Programmed: Ten Commands for a Digital Age*. New York, NY: OR Books, 2010.

Ryan, Julia. "Poll: Teachers Don't Get No Respect." *The Atlantic*, January 24, 2014. https://www.theatlantic.com/education/archive/2014/01/poll-teachers-dont-get-no-respect/283318/.

Semuels, Alana. "Good School, Rich School: Bad School, Poor School." *The Atlantic*, August 25, 2016. https://www.theatlantic.com/business/archive/2016/08 /property-taxes-and-unequal-schools/497333/.

Senge, Peter M. *The Fifth Discipline: The Art and Practice of the Learning Organization*. New York, NY: Currency/Doubleday, 1990.

Shutters, Shade. "Human Society is Totally Interdependent–That's a Huge Advantage, But Also a Huge Survival Risk." *Quartz*, May 2, 2017. https://qz.com/960232/ human-society-is-totally-interdependent-thats-a-huge-advantage-but-also-a-huge -survival-risk/.

Specter, Michael. "Drool: Ivan Pavlov's Real Quest." *The New Yorker*, November 24, 2014. https://www.newyorker.com/magazine/2014/11/24/drool.

State of Massachusetts. "Old Deluder Satan Law of 1647." https://www.mass.gov/file s/documents/2016/08/ob/deludersatan.pdf.

Strauss, Valerie. "Texas GOP Rejects 'Critical Thinking' Skills. Really." *The Washington Post*, July 9, 2012. https://www.washingtonpost.com/blogs/answer -sheet/post/texas-gop-rejects-critical-thinking-skills-really/2012/07/08/gJQA HNpFXW_blog.html.

Tabb, Lloyd. "Great Software Is an Act of Empathy." *lloydtabb*, August 19, 2013. http://lloydtabb.com/great-software-is-an-act-of-empathy.

Turner, Victor. *The Forest of Symbols: Aspects of Ndembu Ritual*. Ithaca, NY: Cornell University Press, 1967.

Tutu, Archbishop Desmond. *Ubuntu Discussion with Students during Semester at Sea 2007*, Posted March 3, 2013 by the Desmond Tutu Peace Foundation. https://www .youtube.com/watch?v=gWZHx9DJR-M, 00:52.

United States Department of Education, National Center for Education Statistics. *Digest of Education Statistics: 2018*. https://nces.ed.gov/programs/digest/d18/.

United States Department of Education, National Center for Education Statistics. "The Condition of Education 2019." *NCES 2019-144*. https://nces.ed.gov/programs/coe/indicator_coj.asp.

United States Department of Education. *For Each and Every Child: A Strategy for Education Equity and Excellence*. Washington, DC: United States Department of Education, 2013. https://www2.ed.gov/about/bdscomm/list/eec/equity-excellence-commission-report.pdf.

van Gannep, Arthur. *The Rites of Passage*. London: Routledge, 1960, reprinted 2004.

Viereck, George Sylvester. "What Life Means to Einstein." *The Saturday Evening Post*, October 26, 1929. https://www.saturdayeveningpost.com/wp-content/uploads/satevepost/what_life_means_to_einstein.pdf.

Vultaggio, Maria. "16 Inspirational Stephen Hawking Quotes About Life, the Universe, and More." *Newsweek*, March 14, 2008. https://www.newsweek.com/stephen-hawking-quote-life-universe-aliens-dead-843692.

Vygotsky, Lev. "The Socialist Alteration of Man." In *Vygotsky Reader*, edited by René van der Veer and Jaan Valsiner. Oxford, UK: Blackwell, 1994.

Wallace, David Foster. *This is Water: Some Thoughts, Delivered on a Significant Occasion, about Living a Compassionate Life*. New York, NY: Little, Brown & Company, 2009.

Wallace-Wells, David. "William Gibson, The Art of Fiction No. 211." *The Paris Review*, Issue 197, Summer 2011. https://www.theparisreview.org/interviews/6089/the-art-of-fiction-no-211-william-gibson.

Whitman, Walt. *Leaves of Grass*. Mount Vernon, NY: Peter Pauper Press, 1891.

Whyte, Jamie. *Crimes Against Logic: Exposing the Bogus Arguments of Politicians, Priests, Journalists, and Other Serial Offenders*. New York, NY: McGraw-Hill, 2005.

Wilford, John Noble. "Earliest Days; Takeoff! How the Wright Brothers Did What No One Else Could." *The New York Times*, December 9, 2003. https://www.nytimes.com/2003/12/09/news/earliest-days-takeoff-how-the-wright-brothers-did-what-no-one-else-could.html.

Yeginsu, Ceylan. "U.K. Appoints a Minister for Loneliness." *The New York Times*, January 17, 2018. https://www.nytimes.com/2018/01/17/world/europe/uk-britain-loneliness.html.

Acknowledgments

This book exists because of the efforts of many, many people. In my attempts to distill and sum up decades of teaching and learning, I am constantly reminded of all the stories I haven't told here. So many people have influenced me and inspired me in one way or another. In particular, in loose chronological order, I'd like to thank:

- My first teachers, my parents Barbara and Gil, and our family who came before. Their DNA, their values, and their resilience flow through me.
- John Wooden, Jim Bruno, Ray Linn, Pansy Rankin, Jerry de Bono, Marty Kravchak, Dave Walbert, Bill Roy, Joe Phillips, Charles Berst, and my other teachers who taught and modeled lessons in character and living that would go on to shape my own students' experiences, because I shamelessly ripped them off.
- Abraham Cabrera, who planted the original seed for this writing project when he rolled up on me in his wheelchair at James Monroe High School in Los Angeles: "Hey Dr. Preston, this ain't like other classes. This is so cool! Are you gonna write a book about this or what?"
- My colleagues in classrooms around the world. If you are a student or a teacher, thank you for all you do every day—you inspire me.
- All of my students who took an ordinary opportunity and did something extraordinary with it.
- Howard Rheingold, Cory Doctorow, Bobby Maximus, Sen. Daylin Leach, Bryan Alexander, and the many other thought leaders and experts who have been willing to spend time online with high school students and share their wisdom.

- Laura Ritchie and her students at the University of Chichester, for being so willing to explore, collaborate, and travel 6,000 miles to share a true love of music and learning.
- My daughter Tara, the most intelligent, wonderful, imaginative, creative, inspiring student I know; my stepson Jace, who constantly encouraged my writing while crafting his own essays for school; and my stepson Brighton, who surfs waves and life with openness and curiosity.
- John Davis, assistant superintendent of Curriculum and Instruction for the Santa Maria Joint Union High School District, for his ongoing support of Open-Source Learning.
- Zolzaya Damdinsuren, the student who invited me to his family's home for dinner—in Ulaan Bataar, Mongolia.
- Gerald Rogers, Julieta Delgadillo, and Kurt Friedmann for reading early drafts and providing feedback.
- Adam Haigler and Ben Owens, for epitomizing Open-Source Learning in their approach to life and work.
- My editors at Rowman & Littlefield, Tom Koerner and Carlie Wall, for believing in the idea and giving the world a book about Open-Source Learning.
- Monica Dunahee, for her knowledge of higher education and attention to detail.
- Harlan Lebo, whose insights on editing, workflow, interviews, digital tools, non-influencers, and the aesthetics of 1970s stereo systems shaped my perspective more than once and made this book what it is.
- My wife Haley, for being my muse, my best friend, my partner in learning and life, and for giving me the time, space, and support I needed between classes and life's many other demands to write this book.

Index

About the Author

David R. Preston, PhD, is an educator, speaker, writer, and consultant who has taught university and K-12 courses for nearly thirty years. David has shared his model of Open-Source Learning with organizations including schools and school districts, colleges and universities, corporations, audiences at the Institute for the Future, the O'Reilly Open Source Conference, TEDxUCLA, and the Royal Geographical Society in London. He continues to teach high school courses and mentor teachers on Open-Source Learning principles. Connect with David at his website, https://davidpreston.net.